THE REFERENCE SHELF

REPRESENTATIVE

AMERICAN SPEECHES

1978-1979

edited by WALDO W. BRADEN
Boyd Professor of Speech
Louisiana State University

THE REFERENCE SHELF

Volume 51   Number 4

THE H. W. WILSON COMPANY

New York 1979

THE REFERENCE SHELF

The books in this series contain reprints of articles, excerpts from books, and addresses on current issues and social trends in the United States and other countries. There are six separately bound numbers in each volume, all of which are generally published in the same calendar year. One number is a collection of recent speeches; each of the others is devoted to a single subject and gives background information and discussion from various points of view, concluding with a comprehensive bibliography. Books in the series may be purchased individually or on subscription.

Library of Congress Catalog Card
Representative American speeches, 1937/38–
  New York, H. W. Wilson Co.
      v. 21. cm. annual. (The Reference shelf)
    Editors: 1937/38–1958/59, A. C. Baird.–1959/60–1969/70.
        L. Thonssen.–1970/71–   W. W. Braden.
 I. American orations.   2. Speeches, addresses, etc.
I. Baird, Albert Craig, ed.   II. Thonssen, Lester,
ed.   III. Braden, Waldo W., ed.   IV. Series.
PS668.B3   815.5082   38–27962

International Standard Book Number 0-8242-0634-7
PRINTED IN THE UNITED STATES OF AMERICA

PREFACE

OVERVIEW OF PUBLIC ADDRESS, 1978–1979

What is the state of public communication in the United States? James Reston, who keeps track of such matters, writes:

> It is one of the cliches of our time that masters of the written and spoken word have vanished from the political world. According to this theory, the talkers have been replaced at the top of governments by tongue-tied technicians. Eloquence is suspect in this complicated and skeptical age, and good speakers are usually losers. (New York *Times*, December 13, 1978.)

The questions of whether eloquence is related to political effectiveness and whether people still regard eloquence as a sign of virtue in their public officials were implicit in the observations of George Bush, as he campaigned around the country for the presidential nomination: "I find that many are losing their confidence in the ability of our leaders —not just in politics but in education, business, and other endeavors—to cope with the problems of our time and to convey a sense of purpose and direction" (see speech of January 25, 1979). Governor Jerry Brown of California, another aspirant for his party's nomination found that "Three-quarters of the people do not trust their government." And still others in the political arena characterize attitudes of the American people toward government as "a crisis in leadership," a failure of nerve, and "a defeatist consensus." These are some of the impressions that our public figures have made on the American populace—their communications have not inspired trust and confidence.

William Safire, political columnist for the New York *Times* and student of "the derivation of political phrases" has suggested that "One reason the political speech is a declining art today is that most modern politicians turn to speech writers for the complete job, and do not collaborate closely in preparation of the expression of what is—or should be—in their own minds" (*Safire's Political Dictionary*, 1978, p XXIX) .

Public address bears the imprint of the times and the seventies have brought cynicism and pessimism, in contrast to the alienation and rebellion of the sixties. The selections in this volume are fraught with censoriousness and dire predictions. Gone is any momentary euphoria that accompanied the bicentennial observances—but the malaise that came in the wake of Watergate continues. Throughout the year public speakers have told listeners that the United States is losing its foreign markets, that the economy is "careening down the path of inflation and recession" (Jerry Brown), that "unchecked growth of federal bureaucracy is a mortal threat to our historic forms of government" (Griffin B. Bell), that Russia is continuing a sinister course in Asia and Africa, and that the oil cartel is wrecking international financial stability. Public figures have also insisted that human rights and freedom of the press are threatened, that caution and government red tape are stifling innovation, that air, land, and water are being polluted by chemicals and waste materials, and that both technology and excessive legalism are consuming us.

These forebodings, presented in unimpressive and easily forgotten speeches, served not to fire the imagination of the voter or spur him to act but to put him in a paralyzed state of indecision. The few heart-warming or enlightening presentations such as the Israeli-Egyptian peace speeches and the Brzezinski defense of our China policy did little to stimulate interest. On the whole, midterm elections during the fall of 1978 did provide a release for much pent-up rhetoric, little of which was inspired or notable. "The desultory campaign," said one reporter, "was generally marked by an absence of serious debate about broad issues" (Norman C. Miller, *Wall Street Journal*, November 9, 1978).

Even expensive media campaigns, designed to attract the voter, produced no dramatic results: fewer than 40 percent of the voters, the smallest number since 1942, turned out to vote, and there was little change in the makeup of the House of Representatives.

As the 1978 presidential aspirants begin to turn up, Democratic dissidents and hopefuls are watching President Carter's popularity slip in the public opinion polls. The persistent question is whether Jimmy Carter can improve his image and credibility in his contacts with the American people and meet the challenges of Senator Edward Kennedy (Massachusetts) and Governor Jerry Brown (California). Both have succeeded in catching the imagination of the public. Brown, in his astounding re-election inaugural address, made a bold political ploy for attention by coming out for a constitutional amendment mandating a balanced federal budget. In contrast to Brown, the charismatic Massachusetts senator has been silent about his presidential intentions.

Smarting from their 1976 defeat, Republicans succeeded in uniting their forces, raising funds, and holding strategy sessions. Leading the cheers were Ronald Reagan, the former governor of California and Gerald Ford, the senior statesman of the party. Representative Phillip M. Crane (Illinois) was first to announce his intention to run, but John Connally and George Bush, both from Texas, were already stumping as possible candidates. Robert Dole (Kansas) announced that he was available and Howard Baker, senator from Tennessee, was attractive to many Republicans.

I have continued to have the good fortune of having the cooperation and help of many persons in completing this volume. The speakers, their assistants and secretaries, program planners, and friends have willingly supplied manuscripts and background materials. My colleagues in the Department of Speech at Louisiana State University have provided good counsel and assistance. The editors have carefully checked my materials, have been most supportive, and have saved me from some embarrassing slips. Of course most important in the project have been Jean Jackson, the departmental secretary, and Myra Fitts, my personal secretary. I am well aware of how much I owe to these persons who have generously supported my efforts.

WALDO W. BRADEN

July, 1979
Baton Rouge, Louisiana

CONTENTS

HUMANE CONCERNS

SOCIAL ATTITUDES AND TECHNOLOGICAL CIVILIZATION [1]

RENÉ DUBOS [2]

"We tend to take a deterministic view of life and history because we overestimate the explanatory power of our knowledge while underestimating the freedom that humans enjoy in making choices and decisions." With these words, René Dubos attempted to lift the spirits and determination of Phi Beta Kappa scholars at Harvard University on June 6, 1978, much as Ralph Waldo Emerson did in his Phi Beta Kappa address in 1837, when he spoke to the contemporary American scholar who faced the complexities of a technological age.

In developing his theme of the two aspects of human life, Dubos cites past humanists and scientists. He is skeptical of those who explain human behavior in terms of "environmental conditioning or other sociobiological processes," which ignore the human elements of instinct, choice, and value. Instead he argues that humanists and scientists should "learn to formulate and develop together" those experiments and goals that would "enlarge and enrich the interplay between humankind and the rest of creation." In other words, technological achievement can be the means by which we can realize worthwhile goals in life. Dubos directs his criticism toward what he considers attitudes of helplessness, resignation, or timidity in facing the problems of our times.

What is reproduced here is an edited version of the address as it appeared in the *American Scholar,* the journal of Phi Beta Kappa (Autumn 1978). When compared with the reading copy, the address is essentially the same except that the first and last paragraphs were added.

A distressing aspect of our times is that so many people of Western civilization have lost their pride in being human, and suffer from a dampening of the spirit that makes

[1] Delivered at Harvard University, June 6, 1978. Reprinted from the *American Scholar,* Volume 47, Number 4, Autumn, 1978. Copyright © 1978 by the United Chapters of Phi Beta Kappa. By permission of the publishers.
[2] For biographical note, see Appendix.

them doubt our ability to deal with the future. This common frailty appears the more painful when one compares it with the confident mood of the eighteenth century.

In 1743, Benjamin Franklin offered his fellow Americans "A Proposal for Promoting Useful Knowledge Among the British Plantations in America." He had in mind an academy organized for discussions and experiments that would, he hoped, "let Light into the Nature of Things, tend to increase the Power of Man over Matter, and multiply the Conveniences or Pleasure of Life." Franklin's concept eventually resulted in the creation of the American Philosophical Society, which finally obtained its charter in 1780. The wording of Franklin's proposal and of the American Philosophical Society's charter reflect pride in being human and confidence that human life can be improved by knowledge. This sense of pride and confidence was characteristic of the eighteenth-century Enlightenment but has become much weaker in our times. I want to discuss here the effect of social attitudes on the development of technological civilization but find it necessary to express first some of my views concerning human nature.

The shape of the modern world has been largely determined by the philosophers of the Enlightenment. Among them, none has been more influential than Voltaire and Jean Jacques Rousseau, both of whom died in Paris two hundred years ago in 1778.

Voltaire and Rousseau had spent their lives in France and Switzerland, except for a few years in England; both associated with Diderot and the other encyclopedists; both had acquired literary fame early in life and had been lionized in the French salons by men and women of wealth and influence. Despite this commonality of social conditioning, however, they developed in adulthood opposite attitudes concerning ways of life and views of humankind.

Voltaire believed in reason—always. He was convinced that humankind could be enlightened and improved by pure intellectuality and by putting wit at the service of strong logic. Although sickly during most of his life, he derived much pleasure from his social contacts and from the fortune he accumulated. In contrast, Rousseau had little faith in reason. He trusted instead in feelings and in passionate action dictated by the heart. His vision was in many ways unsophisticated and his social life became increasingly limited. Through choices they made early in life, Voltaire and Rousseau thus came to symbolize two opposite aspects of French civilization and of human life—the cult of reason and the worship of instincts.

Among artists, Thomas Rowlandson and William Blake constitute other examples of similarities and contrasts. Both died in 1827 at seventy years of age. Both were Londoners, respectively the sons of a wool merchant and a hosier. Both studied painting at the Royal Academy, proclaimed the superiority of line over volume, and used watercolor as their preferred medium. Neither artist accepted the world for what it was, and each in his own way used painting as a vehicle for his social ideas. Yet, while having all these things in common, the two men had a very different view of life. Rowlandson, the gambler, depicted society with the cynical art of the caricaturist. William Blake, the poet and idealist, perceived and expressed creation with the bright-eyed innocence of a child.

René Descartes and Blaise Pascal were two scientists of the same period who also presented striking resemblances and contrasts. Both were born in prosperous, highly cultivated families in the legal profession in the French provinces; both exhibited early in life great gifts in the sciences and especially in mathematics; both achieved international fame and were socially feted—yet they developed opposite intellectual attitudes. Descartes became more and more convinced that all aspects of creation, including human nature, would eventually be understood through the use of reason and analytical processes. Pascal, in contrast, appealed increasingly to faith as the only valid approach to knowledge and concluded that the heart has reasons that the rational mind cannot possibly know.

These examples make me skeptical of attempts to explain human behavior by environmental conditioning or other sociobiological processes. Human life is of course influenced by genetic and environmental factors, but the really interesting aspects of life—those that make humans so obviously different from animals—clearly transcend such primitive biological explanations. Behaviorists and sociobiologists can account for the animal aspects of human life but have little of interest to say concerning the choices that make us transcend our animality. Artists and other humanists are skilled in the perception and description of human traits but are no more able than scientists to predict what a particular person would like to become or wants to do at a particular time. All human beings live, as it were, in worlds of their own, never completely accessible to other persons.

Thus, human nature is not so simple that it can be reduced to the knowledge of twentieth-century scholars. Humanists and scientists have contributed much to the understanding of our characteristics, our origins, and our potentialities. As specialists, however, we are prone to suffer from a peculiar kind of infantilism that makes us regard the phenomena studied in our own discipline as the most important for the understanding of human nature. We tend to take a deterministic view of life and history because we overestimate the explanatory power of our knowledge while underestimating the freedom that humans enjoy in making choices and decisions.

Admittedly, free will cannot be proven, let alone explained, but this failure does not weigh much against the countless manifestations of freedom in everyday life. What Samuel Johnson wrote in 1778 is still just as true in 1978: "All theory is against the freedom of the will, all experience for it." The most important aspects of human nature are not necessarily those that can be explained by contemporary knowledge. Human beings—and most likely animals also—constantly choose and decide in a way that makes a mockery of orthodox biological and social determinism.

The deterministic view of human fate has been recently strengthened by the widespread assumption that technology —or rather what Jacques Ellul calls *la technique*—is now entirely governed by objective science and has developed an internal logic of its own which is almost independent of human control. Yet it is obvious that human choices continue to influence all aspects of technological societies, as they have always influenced other human institutions. The rapid changes in architectural fashions during recent decades provide visual evidence of the fact that human caprice plays a dominant role in the use of modern technology for the design of buildings. For example, architects are now advocating a change from "modernism" to "post modernism," not by reason of new technologies or new social concepts, but simply because of a desire for change. "Less is More" was the motto of designers of a generation ago. The phrase "Less is Bore" is now considered sufficient justification for change.

In 1605, at the very beginning of the scientific era, Francis Bacon wrote in the *Advancement of Learning* that "The invention of the mariner's needle which giveth the direction is of no less benefit for navigation than the invention of the sails which giveth the motion." This was a clear warning that technological progress would depend on the formulation of goals as much as on the development of techniques. Admittedly, Bacon's warning did not have much influence until recently because most technologists have been more eager for motion than concerned with direction, but there is evidence that the social mood is beginning to change. While bigness and speed are still the most widely accepted criteria of success, we have come to realize that the word progress means only moving forward, as likely as not on the wrong road.

The change in public attitude can be seen in the light

of an event that occurred less than half a century ago. In 1933, the city of Chicago held a World's Fair to celebrate the "Century of Progress" which had elapsed since its birth in 1833 and which had seen the triumph of scientific technology. The organizers of the Fair were so convinced that scientific technology invariably improves human life that they stated in the guidebook, "Science discovers, genius invents, industry applies, and *man adapts himself to* or is *molded by* new things." One of the subtitles of the guidebook was "Science Finds, Industry Applies, Man *Conforms*" (italics mine). This philosophy was still dominant among the futurologists of the 1950s when they tried to forecast what the world would be like in the year 2000. With dismal uniformity, they envisioned a future shaped by far-out technologies and architectures, without relevance to human needs or to natural conditions.

A fundamental change of attitude occurred during the 1960s and 1970s. No one would dare state today that humans must conform to technological imperatives or that they will be molded by technological forces. We want instead that industrial development be adapted to humankind and to nature—not the other way around, as was advocated by the organizers of the Chicago Fair. This new attitude, based on human and ecological criteria, will determine the role played by knowledge and technology in the future.

Charles Lindbergh's life, as reported in his posthumously published *Autobiography of Values,* symbolizes how the modern world has evolved from fascination with sophisticated technologies to the realization that unwise and excessive dependence on these technologies threatens fundamental human values. While on a camping trip in Kenya during his late adult life, Lindbergh had become intoxicated with the sensate qualities of African life which he perceived "in the dances of the Masai, in the prolificacy of the Kikuyu, in the nakedness of boys and girls. You feel these qualities in the sun on your face and the dust on your feet . . . in the yelling of the hyenas and the bark of zebras." Experiencing these sensate qualities made Lindbergh ask himself, "Can it be that civilization is detrimental to human progress? . . . Does civilization eventually become such an overspecialized development of the intellect, so organized and artificial, so separated from the senses that it will be incapable of continued functioning?"

Lindbergh's doubts concerning civilization were the more surprising to me because, in the 1930s, I had known him as a colleague in the laboratories of the Rockefeller Institute for Medical Research, where he was developing an organ perfusion pump in collaboration with Dr. Alexis Carrel. His dominant interest at that time was, along with aviation, mechanical devices to explore what he calls in his book "the mechanics of life." His *Autobiography of Values* reveals how he eventually moved from an exclusive interest in the mechanical applications of science to a deep concern for its social and philosophical implications. He remained enamored of modern science and was, for example, fascinated by space exploration, but became increasingly distraught at seeing technology used for trivial and destructive ends.

Thus, Bacon at the beginning of the scientific era, and Lindbergh more than two centuries later, expressed in different words a concern which has become central to our form of civilization. Science and technology provide us with the *means* to create almost anything we want, but the development of means without worthwhile *goals* generates at best a dreary life and may at worst lead to tragedy. Some of the most spectacular feats of scientific technology call to mind Captain Ahab's words in Melville's *Moby-Dick:* "All my means are sane, my purpose and my goals mad." The demonic force, however, is not scientific technology itself, but our propensity to consider means as ends—an attitude symbolized by the fact that we measure success by the gross national product rather than by the quality of life and of the environment.

Many spectacular achievements of our times are the current manifestations of trends initiated several decades ago. We have advanced civilization chiefly by accelerating and magnifying the process of change, often to the point of absurdity. One motorcar contributes to freedom; one hundred million motorcars not only generate traffic jams but also constitute evidence of addiction. Industrial energy in small doses makes life easier and more diversified; complete dependence on industrial energy becomes a form of slavery.

Vigor has been more characteristic of our age than concern for values. But there are indications that the near future may be shaped by more humane attitudes. An awareness is in the air that doing more and more of what we are now doing, only bigger and faster, is not for the sane, and that we can get our means and ends straight only by inquiring into the long-range consequences of our activities.

Innovations can be lastingly successful only if they are adapted to the invariants of physical and human nature. Fortunately, such constraints are compatible with much diversity, because there are different ways to function in agreement with natural laws. The individuality of a culture is achieved through the choices made by humans among the options available to them at a given time in a given place. Until recently, these options were provided almost exclusively by the natural world and choices were made by caprice or empirical wisdom, but options and choices are now increasingly affected by knowledge, especially scientific knowledge. Knowledge enlarges the range of options through different mechanisms. It provides information that can enter the public domain in the form of verifiable facts and laws. It generates technological innovations that can serve chosen ends. It constantly surprises and subverts because its findings and uses are largely unpredictable, thus making people more receptive to new attitudes and more willing to change their ways.

However, while knowledge increases the range of options, it cannot be the sole basis for decision making because it is always incomplete and therefore cannot describe all aspects of the world that bear on human life and on environmental quality. Knowledge is more effective as a generator of possibilities than as a guide to choice and a source of ethics.

Most natural ecosystems, for example, are extremely resilient. Landscapes and waterscapes that had been badly damaged by pollution or misuse have spontaneously regained ecological health when the causes of the damage have been removed. But ecological health is compatible with different ecological states which correspond to different cultural values. The temperate zone, for example, was covered with forests and marshes before the advent of agriculture, and the forest spontaneously returns as soon as farming is discontinued. Professional ecologists tend to believe that we should take advantage of this resiliency and let nature recreate a forested landscape similar to that of the original wilderness. According to my taste and judgment, however, a diversified landscape of cultivated fields, meadows, and woodlands is ecologically and economically more desirable, as well as aesthetically more attractive, than the primeval forested wilderness. For this reason, I welcome the efforts that are being made in several parts of the temperate zone to limit the growth of brush and trees where agriculture has been abandoned, even though open fields are not natural ecosystems since they are of human origin.

Ancient Greece also was covered with forests. The present Greek landscape is the consequence of erosion following deforestation but, as in other parts of the world, trees spontaneously come back in areas which are protected against browsing by goats and rabbits. While erosion has disastrous agricultural consequences, it has the merit of enabling, in my eyes, light to play its bewitching game on the white framework of Attica. I like to believe that the tormented divinities of the preclassical Greek period may have become more playful and human when they emerged from the darkness of the forest into the luminous open landscape. Logic might not have flourished in Greece if the land had remained covered with an entangling opaque vegetation.

Resources do not exist as such in nature. They are created by knowledge and technology which make it possible to separate certain substances from the raw materials in which they are present in the natural state, and to transform them so that they can be used to some chosen end. The bauxite from which aluminum is now prepared did not become a resource until a century ago when technologies became available to separate the metal from this ore and to tool it for metallurgical purposes. Similarly, oil, gas, and uranium became resources only after technologies had been developed to extract them and use them as sources of energy.

Although our form of civilization depends upon abundant supplies of metals and energy, opinions differ as to the priority of these resources in the social system of values. Enormous reserves of copper exist in the Cascades National Park, but their exploitation would require a huge open mine and would thus spoil a wonderful wilderness area. Titanium could be obtained from the sand of Cape Cod, and various other metals as well as uranium from the granite of the White Mountains, but this would damage the aesthetic quality of these humanized landscapes. Thus, the "limits to growth" are determined, not only by the existence of raw materials but also by the choices society makes concerning the various factors affecting the quality of life.

The supplies of fossil fuels will eventually be depleted but practical techniques will certainly be developed within a few decades to produce energy from renewable sources—nuclear or solar or probably both. The selection of methods for the production of energy will involve, however, choices based not only on scientific knowledge and cost-benefit analysis, but also on judgments of value concerning the ideal form of society.

Technologies for the production and utilization of nuclear energy will inevitably involve enormous generators that will require strict technological and social controls, resulting in a high degree of organization and centralization. In contrast, the first steps in the use of solar energy will have to be carried out in fairly small units—a necessity that will lead to social decentralization. Many persons, perhaps the great majority, will prefer to have abundant electricity on tap without giving thought to its origin, its environmental effects, and its indirect social costs. Other persons will favor instead small-scale technologies more compatible with social decentralization and with regional and cultural pluralism. The final outcome will probably be a mix of centralized and decentralized sources of energy, selected to fit the environmental and social characteristics of a given area, and compatible with the expression of the multiple aspects of human nature.

Two hundred years ago the act incorporating the American Philosophical Society began with the statement that "the cultivation of useful knowledge, and the advancement of the liberal arts and sciences in any Country, have the most direct tendency towards the improvement of agriculture, the enlargement of trade, the ease and comfort of life, the ornament of society, and the increase and happiness of mankind." We have gone far toward fulfilling the scientific and technological aspects of Franklin's proposal but have not contributed much to the "ornament of society" or to human happiness. We are much better at developing means than at formulating ends, as for example when we create sophisticated means of communication but use them to transmit trivialities or when we increase productivity of certain goods while neglecting the experiences that could be derived from what is being produced. The most difficult and important problems relate to questions of values. As Bacon stated in 1605, direction is at least as important as motion.

The relation between means and ends, however, is far

more complex than appears from the contrast between the two words. Exalted ends are often the ultimate expressions of means developed for minor uses or even for their own sake. No one is born with a biological need for writing or reading, and many societies have indeed gotten along well without these skills. But once writing had been invented—probably first in Sumer to keep records of supplies—it generated ends unrelated to its first use and became a creator of new values. To a large extent, the growth of civilization depends upon the possibility of formulating new ends that become attainable because new means are available.

Ends thus evolve with the means created by civilization, in our time particularly by science and technology. But ends are desirable only to the extent that they contribute worthwhile values to life and to the earth. In this light, the difference between means and ends, although often blurred, is nevertheless real. Ends refer to the quality of the experience, means to the techniques that can be used to enlarge and enrich this experience. Ends might be regarded as the domain of the humanities, means as that of the sciences. Western civilization will not be really successful until its humanists and scientists learn to formulate and develop together, as advocated by Franklin in 1743, "philosophical experiments" that enlarge and enrich the interplay between humankind and the rest of creation.

In 1837, Emerson concluded his famous Phi Beta Kappa oration with a plea that the American scholar strive for independence from European models. I would submit that the most important task for the American scholar today is to achieve the integration of the sciences and the humanities.

SIMPLE JUSTICE AND EXISTENTIAL VICTIMS[1]

WILLIAM J. McGILL[2]

In recent years, the emergence of special interest groups has upset the traditional party structure of American politics and made the creation of a national policy increasingly difficult. In the fall elections of 1978, the single-issue lobbies were able to influence several elections.

As a close observer of social and political ferment in New York City, Dr. William J. McGill, president of Columbia University, has been concerned with excessive strength of advocacy groups in our society. He compares the tactics and emotional appeal of adversary constituency groups to those of labor unions and notes that their "criterion of success is not necessarily the public good or the achievement of social harmony, but the advancement of the special interests of one's own constituency by any means not specifically prohibited."

On October 6, 1978, Dr. McGill delivered the 35th Robert Houghwart Jackson Memorial Lecture before the National Judicial College, the Judicial College Building, at the University of Nevada, Reno. He spoke at the conclusion of the General Jurisdiction Course to an audience composed of state trial judges. Other speakers to address similar sessions throughout the year included Chief Justice C. William O'Neill of the Supreme Court of Ohio, Dean Norval Morris of the University of Chicago Law School, and Judge A. Leon Higginbotham Jr. of the US Court of Appeals, Philadelphia.

The endowed institution, established in 1954, is composed "of judges, by judges, and for judges." Each year it conducts a series of resident sessions on subjects connected with the administration of justice. "In 1978 the College conducted 35 resident sessions. . . . This year was the first time all 50 states were represented in these programs, as well as the District of Columbia, military, United States possessions and territories, foreign, Indian Tribal, federal appellate, administrative law, as well as court personnel" (*News* of the National Judicial College). A total of 1,226

[1] Delivered before the Judicial College, at the Judicial College Building, on the University of Nevada campus, Reno, Nevada, October 6, 1978. Quoted by permission.

[2] For biographical note, see Appendix.

certificates of completion of sessions were issued during the twelve months.

Recognizing the sophistication of his audience of judges, McGill chose to clothe his hard-hitting analysis of the social and legal aspects of our "adversary society" in a philosophical context. The reader should understand McGill's premise in using the term "existential victimization": "Man's attempt to find meaning and identity in a universe of overwhelming complexity threatening to annihilate him is one of the central problems of existential philosophy." He maintains that victims of urban pressures "adopt a neurotic mode of adaptation best described as an emotional commitment to the role of victim" and that when they are unable to develop inner resources to cope with frustration, they become "easy marks for manipulation by demagogues and revolutionaries." He directly addressed those in his audience who face the results of these urban pressures day after day in their courts.

During the twentieth century our nation has become an object of growing awe and apprehension in the eyes of the rest of the world. We are the world's foremost industrial colossus, and also its most flamboyant democracy. America's special genius for sharing the fruits of its labor as well as for spectacular internal conflict has produced a phenomenon unique in history. It is certainly the case that the economic and political institutions of the United States continue to evolve in ways not fully anticipated by our founding fathers.

Our industrial system came to full flower after World War I simultaneously with the spread of Marxist ideology, socialism, and state planning to Eastern Europe, Asia, and Africa. Modern America is built upon the highest standards of technological advancement and also upon the stabilizing effects of an affluent working class. American workers have created their high standard of living via a remarkably productive form of labor-management bargaining that seems to offer the most serious alternative to Marxism in the world today. European and Japanese democracies borrow heavily upon our industrial and marketing methods. They have also managed to do very well for themselves by selling to markets that we have created. All this accounts for the awe.

We are viewed equally with apprehension. America's foreign policy wavers between extremes of dreadful naivete and utter callousness—from advocacy of unilateral disarmament and the golden rule, to CIA-sponsored "destabilization" of other governments. America's economy swings up and down with the secular trends and occasional wild gyrations of the market place. Such fluctuations send shivers all over the globe because for more than thirty years the foreign policy of the United States and our currency have stabilized not only the economies of Western Europe and Japan, but most of the Third World as well. When the United States goes off into a political or economic spasm, anxiety is bound to be felt almost immediately in every corner of the world.

This traditional mixture of awe and apprehension has become greatly magnified in recent times as our nation moved unexpectedly into a remarkable and almost revolutionary period of social change beginning early in the 1960s. No one can say with any assurance where this new era will take us, and when or whether its current ferment will diminish, but what is happening seems plain enough.

The steps taken originally in the mid-1950s putting an end to school segregation in the United States blossomed into full fledged civil rights activism on behalf of blacks during the decade which followed. The methods worked out by America's black people for achieving their civil liberties involved a unique combination of group psychology, legislative and regulatory initiative, legal maneuver, and extremely clever handling of the mass media. Very quickly these new methods generated virtually unbearable pressures on traditional institutions to align themselves with the demands of a newly assertive black leadership.

During two extraordinary decades we have been privileged to witness the construction of a black political constituency right before our eyes. It is now a force of major importance in American life as the last presidential election showed. The realities of racism and unequal opportunity in the United States moved rapidly from the status of

sensitive matters never discussed in polite circles, to potent
arguments used by articulate blacks in the most public way
to demonstrate the unfair treatment accorded to black
people in America. Hence change was accomplished not by
the discovery of a conscience in the United States but by the
introduction of new psychological, sociological, and legal
methods for achieving human rights; methods that have
proved to be remarkably effective.

Other sensitive constituencies: Spanish speaking minori-
ties, native Americans, women, environmentalists, consumer
advocates, students, homosexuals, the handicapped, and
senior citizens, began to think of themselves as capable of
improving their own standing in American life by becoming
politically active and availing themselves of the techniques
of social change pioneered by American blacks. These new
constituencies called upon the same psychological methods
for developing group consciousness. They turned to the
same legal remedies and made full use of the publicity
techniques developed by an earlier black leadership in the
civil rights movement.

Concern for human rights among young people of college age in the United States became greatly intensified
during the VietNam years. A generally successful adaptation of the dramatic techniques of mass protest and media
publicity pioneered in the civil rights movement was undertaken in support of initiatives aimed at reshaping the government's war policy. The Nixon administration's attempt
to roll back the tide of human rights in America and to
reinstate earlier methods of social control, collapsed in the
storms of the Watergate scandal. The paranoia and emotional hostility brought to bear against Mr. Nixon during
Watergate will, I believe, be viewed by future historians as
one of the landmarks in the social history of the United
States. The dynamics shaping Watergate into an explosion
powerful enough to unseat a President, must have been
closely related to the idealism and emotional commitment
of the civil rights movement.

As a consequence of the disgrace of Nixonian revanch-ism, human rights ferment now continues at fever pitch in the United States. New constituencies appear almost monthly. Within the last two years we have seen the emergence of gay people, the handicapped, and the elderly as organized constituencies each with a special psychological identity and each with its own agenda for social change.

Once again dramatic conflict, this time on behalf of human rights and the special interests of a multitude of small constituencies in the United States, has created amazement and awe throughout the world. Others wonder as they watch us how we can absorb all these unprecedented strivings without tearing ourselves apart.

Attempts at assessment of the scope and meaning of the multifaceted human rights political phenomenon in the United States today are bound to be hazardous. In the first place it is too soon. We are still in the fever of the process. Moreover, speculation runs the risk of denunciation by committed advocates who will feel that any attempt at analysis of their methods is motivated by hostility and hence must be a mask for reviving the Nixon administration's attempts to roll back civil liberties in America. We are lacking the cold light of history for assessing the full mean-ing of the extraordinary social phenomena we have been experiencing.

Yet speculation is necessary if we are to arrive at even an elementary understanding of our own time. I certainly believe that this human rights ferment is not merely an ideological phenomenon. Although it has a powerful philo-sophical foundation in our ideals of social justice, it also manifests a great deal of artful methodology. For instance, we might begin with a frank recognition that the civil rights movement succeeded in the United States not only because of its idealism and commitment, but also because its emotional driving forces were buttressed by concepts of organization, bargaining methods, and techniques of con-flict resolution closely related to those evolved by organized labor during the 1930s. I do not believe it to be very far from the mark to consider the multiplicity of human rights constituencies now active in the country as conceptually similar to labor unions. Both areas, labor law and civil rights law, create similar group entities with narrow psychological boundaries—"the union" and "the constituency." They utilize closely related pressure tactics and similar types of grievance machinery. Both areas make extensive use of the adversary system of Anglo-American law for the management of bargaining between groups and for the resolution of disputes.

In an adversary system the client's interest is pursued to the disregard of nearly all other considerations. Hence the criterion of success is not necessarily the public good or the achievement of social harmony, but the advancement of the special interests of one's own constituency by any means not specifically prohibited. American political theory holds that the struggle of advocacies, guided by legislation defining the rights of all parties, and monitored by an impartial judicial process, will lead to fair decisions ultimately beneficial to society. Hence the fierce and sometimes frightening rhetoric of newly organized constituencies—women, native Americans, and gay people, for example—is perfectly understandable as the use of an adversary system developed in labor law but now employed on behalf of constituency interests in the field of human rights.

The emergence of such constituency groups organized on a national scale in forms resembling labor unions, and the cautious adjustments of politicians seeking not to offend important constituencies, are major new developments in American society. The nature of our politics, dominated by two broad-gauged political parties, fosters the growth of constituency groups once they demand recognition. Legislatures listen to and attempt to work with these constituency groups in proportion to their potential voting power. The pattern was originally laid down by organized labor in advancing the candidacies of politicians friendly to labor whatever their party affiliations might be. Since the 1930s, a whole generation of politicians has developed whose expectations for reelection were dependent upon organized labor support. In the 1970s politicians are forced to thread their way through a veritable minefield of contentious issues posed by a multitude of national constituencies. Politicians must be publicly answerable to such groups and yet still manage to maintain a broad base of voter support. The ability of organized labor to deliver the vote in these pluralistic circumstances is no longer guaranteed. Nevertheless, it was the labor movement which pioneered the symbiotic relation between elected politicians and organized constituencies within the framework of our two-party system.

In human rights politics the linkage between constituencies and political action has produced a modern American political phenomenon known as the "caucus." We find caucuses everywhere and in a variety of forms: the black caucus, the women's caucus, the environmental caucus, the senior citizens' caucus, and so on. A caucus is perhaps best understood as the political arm of a constituency group. It is similar in concept to the political action committee of a labor union, and it operates in much the same fashion, setting forth policy objectives and punishing or rewarding politicians as a consequence of their willingness to work toward these objectives.

Great importance should be attached to improved understanding of these uniquely American social and political phenomena. I am attempting to describe them dispassionately, neither sympathetically as an advocate of social change, nor critically as an agent of an establishment university. It appears to me that we are well along the road toward building one of the most interesting and undistilled adversary societies the world has yet seen. It is almost the complete antithesis of the ideological simplicity and monolithic politics characteristic of the Marxist states. While we have retained the structure of broad-gauged political governance under two political parties, it is also true that beneath this broad umbrella there is a furious clash of pressures among innumerable organized constituencies, labor groups, political action groups, racial and ethnic groups, social and religious groups, consumer and environmental groups, all well-organized and bashing heads continuously. It is an incredible, noisy brawl, full of rhetorical threats, strikes, sit-ins, investigations, lawsuits, and all the pressure tactics that have become familiar on the American political scene.

The mass media are crucial to the functioning of this pressure system because newspapers and television provide the principal means by which this multitude of constituency groups organize themselves, contend with one another, and attempt via their rhetorical displays to influence the Congress and the public. As the number of constituency groups increases, more dramatic ingenuity and more flamboyant rhetoric must be developed in order to attract headlines. The principal weapon available to protesting constituencies is not really the threat of riotous physical violence which abounds in their rhetoric. The real weapon is more likely to be pressure-packed demonstrations aimed at media coverage, all of it intended to be acutely embarrassing to the government or other established institutions toward which grievances are directed. Coverage is assured because conflict sells newspapers, and especially because the David-Goliath relation between human rights constituencies and large institutions conforms to one of the basic requirements of news. Hence the constituency needs only to project human drama and emotion into its protest tactics in order to be assured of sympathetic media treatment.

Much of our social policy then emerges as the vector resultant of a complex struggle of narrowly-based constituency groups, each acting in its own interest and bargaining for special advantage with government and with established institutions. The abortion struggle and the national campaign against nuclear energy facilities, now very active in the United States, illustrate the phenomena of the adversary constituency system I am describing. Neither campaign is characterized by calm, rational argument. Instead we are treated to a flood of bizarre rhetoric and media-oriented demonstrations, organized for frankly political objectives by fairly small constituencies. The large amount of coverage given to these demonstrations is determined by the emotional interest which they generate and by the dramatic impact of their tactics.

We are living through one of the most remarkable periods of our history. This bewildering struggle of advocacy groups in the United States is producing amazement elsewhere in the world. The amazement is partly admiration for the creativity of our political system, and partly apprehension that we may one day tear ourselves apart in the enthusiasm of our contentiousness. I hope that I am not alone in expressing concern about the psychological stresses current in the United States in consequence of such unfiltered advocacy on behalf of a plethora of noisy constituencies.

Alexander Solzhenitsyn in his now-famous commencement speech at Harvard this past spring [June 8, 1978] delivered a powerful attack upon the weakness, materialism and excessive legalism of western society. His voice carried overtones reminiscent of Gibbon's critique of imperial Rome. Solzhenitsyn's criticisms of the West were almost brutal in their candor, but as an observer whose vantage point lies behind a high fence in a remote area of northern New England, he does seem to me to misunderstand the complexity and depth of American life. An important part of Solzhenitsyn's stress on weakness and excessive legalism is translatable into my own concern over the growth of legalistic adversary struggle among narrowly-based constituency groups, and I believe that Solzhenitsyn is right on target.

But one also needs to have survived for a decade in a volatile urban area attempting to manage a large institution under conditions of continuing threat and struggle if one is to understand the unusual complexity of the forces

at work in today's America. The urban struggle has material objectives and it is viciously competitive. Nevertheless,
it is not essentially materialistic nor does it manifest weakness. Something powerful is being fought out in our cities.
It is almost a war of survival among individuals and institutions. It breeds immense capability in the survivors,
and even more strength among those who manage to stand
above the struggle directing their concerns not just to the
interests of their own narrow constituencies but to the
welfare of all the people.

For more than eight years at Columbia University I have
witnessed and participated in the competitive struggles associated with the challenging conditions of life in New York
City: man against the system, citizen against City Hall,
tenant against landlord, consumer against Con Edison, student against the administration, community against the
University. There are just too many people competing for
too few goods and services. It is too easy for us to get in
each other's way. As a consequence almost no public in-
teraction is either simple or pleasant. It seems perfectly
apparent that a great many people are unable to bear the
stresses of such continuous infighting, and of course the
number of hardy survivors who not only manage successfully but also rise above their own narrow concerns, can be
numbered on the fingers of one's hand.

I have grown increasingly impressed by the insight contributed by existential thought to the social and legal problems posed by the innumerable and endlessly frustrating
struggles characterizing modern urban life. Man's attempts
to find meaning and identity in a universe of overwhelming
complexity threatening to annihilate him is one of the central problems of existential philosophy. It has fascinated the
academic world since the issues were first set forth by the
Danish philosopher, Soren Kierkegaard, early in the Nineteenth Century. Existential problems are certainly nothing
abstract in New York City. They are also experienced daily
by millions of individuals in other urban areas. I have had

an unparalleled opportunity to study the existential difficulties posed by the tough urban environment surrounding Columbia University. I find it surprising that there has been so little critical discussion of this material in academic and legal circles. Much of the social and legal theory setting forth the nature of grievances in modern American life seems to me not to be based on systematic observation of the existential quality of urban social conditions, but rather on the preconceived notion that grievances widely perceived as real by members of a social group must be traceable to real injustices in relations among groups or between individuals and institutions.

My own observation is that many people break under persistent existential stress; in my experience perhaps one-quarter to one-third of the population of large urban centers such as New York City. They then adopt a neurotic mode of adaptation best described as an emotional commitment to the role of victim. Such victimization absolves them of the requirement for further struggle against a difficult and unyielding environment. They satisfy themselves that they have been crushed by overwhelming and insensitive opposition, that life is hopeless and unbearable. They give up their own goals in life, spending instead an appreciable part of their time explaining to all who will listen the injuries and injustices that have been worked upon them. I see hundreds of these crippled people daily on the upper West Side of Manhattan. They constitute an appreciable portion of the faces in the crowd at protest meetings and demonstrations. Most of them are easy marks for manipulation by demagogues and revolutionaries.

There is no doubt at all, in my judgment, about the rapid growth of the phenomenon of existential victimization with all its attendant neuroticism in the population of New York City and other large urban areas during the last 30 years. Nowhere is it more evident than in the rhetoric of the municipal labor unions. The experience of watching and listening to a policeman carrying a picket sign and telling of the horrors of his life, is one that I will not soon forget. Existential victimization seems to be an important idea in accounting for the unusually rapid expansion of demand for new social services in our major cities. The process of psychological victimization seems to feed on a population, creating exaggerated forms of dependency and hence unprecedented demands for social services. Estimates of the required level of support are never really testable except in circumstances of genuine crisis, as for example, in wartime, when people are forced to survive under stress or die in neglect. At such times we come to understand in all its ugly reality what is actually required for survival. The enormous gap between this bare minimum and the perceived need for services in an urban population under existential stress, defines an immense and almost insoluble problem. It is also a problem whose importance cannot be overstated. Many of our current social policies seem to me not directed toward the goal of a productive society offering maximum opportunity for self-realization. They are directed instead at alleviating a wide range of perceived grievances and perceived tensions via increased benefits, special legal protections, and improved social services. The cost of such policies is measured not in money alone but in exaggerated forms of dependency.

In modern America we must begin to devise social policies and concepts of public need that are genuinely humane to those genuinely in want, but that are not also so attractive as to foster uncontrollable growth of the victimization phenomenon. No one knows with any precision where this line should be drawn. It is a social issue of staggering complexity on which universities have not been nearly as helpful as they should have been in illuminating the subtleties. Accordingly, under great political pressure, we have tended in recent years to overprovide, ignoring the danger of increasing numbers of dependent, neurotic victims.

And so Solzhenitsyn believes that we are weak. How could Alexander Solzhenitsyn who singlehandedly fought off the concentrated power of the Soviet Union by the discipline and strength of his own character, who managed to survive Siberia, work camps, and the secret police; how could he understand the psychology of the existential victim?

I am convinced that existential victimization offers a fertile culture in which the human rights movements of the future will grow, securing new adherents, and grasping for political power. You should read the recent work of Cloward and Piven [*Poor People's Movement: Why They Succeed, How They Fail*] on Welfare rights if you are skeptical of this view. The framers of our growing body of human rights laws and associated administrative regulations have proceeded from the most idealistic motives in attempting to protect the weak, and to correct injustices. In fact we must all be committed to the removal of all real injustice from American life. There is no basis on which the continuance of discrimination or the denial of civil liberties can be either justified or excused. However, I also believe that the psychological appeals of human rights groups and the affirmative steps required by the growing body of human rights law especially those involving special protections and special services to be applied toward the alleviation of group tensions and group grievances, must be thought through very carefully. The central ideas developed in legislation and administrative regulations thus far have been limited to the alleviation of grievances and the correction of past injustices. DeTocqueville once observed that "it would seem as if every imagination in the United States were—to invent means of increasing the wealth and satisfying the wants of the public." In our own time this responsiveness to public demand has led to a significant number of actions aimed at reducing tensions and redressing grievances which may also have encouraged the proliferation of existential victimization in the very constituencies we are attempting to help. Legislation on health services for the aged and the poor developed during the last fifteen years

is a prime example. It may well have worked to weaken
not to heal. One of the sad and seldom-stated truths about
the evil of discrimination is that extreme care is required
in the measures employed for its correction. Otherwise we
lay ourselves open to a cancerous growth of existential victimization all across the society.

If then, the leadership of the human rights movement
remains strong and if its characteristics as a quasi-labor
movement are used to achieve a continuing and carefully
analyzed improvement of conditions for our minority constituencies leading to a more just society, we must be sensitive and responsive to such idealism. If, on the other hand,
this body of law and social practice becomes an instrument
for encouraging the development of increasing numbers of
social victims, bereft of dignity, unwilling or unable to help
themselves, dependent upon support services whose cost is
borne by decreasing numbers in the population, America's
survival power will be damaged in a hostile world environment. We need to be able to tell the difference between
what is just, and what creates existential victimization. Unfortunately, it is a rather subtle difference not easily ascer-
tainable in a cacophony of advocative rhetoric.

The logic of the position outlined thus far is that any
group seeking to advance the interests of its members has
the option of attempting to establish itself as still another
vocal constituency to which society must pay special attention. During the past two decades a wealth of experience
has been built up on the artful use of media-oriented pressure and publicity methods. Such techniques are readily
available, for example, to physicians, churches, the academic world, even the judiciary. Moreover, an argument
can be made that only by such means can one's voice be
heard in the chorus of advocacy now abroad in America.
I will not advance such an argument. Quite the contrary,
having also pointed to the phenomenon of existential victimization in urban life and the danger which a growing

number of psychological victims poses to the health of our social order, I will take a rather different approach.

In New York City during eight crucial years at Columbia, it has struck me repeatedly that some form of leadership beyond the mere articulation of existential despair is necessary for the future well-being of urban life. Obviously we must console the victims among us, and we must treat them gently. But we must also begin to search for the moral dignity that emerges from a sheer determination to struggle against a difficult and unyielding environment, to carry on even when there are no easy solutions to the problems that must be solved.

What America needs most of all at this moment in its history is a deeper understanding of itself and a determined effort at self-healing. Where are the agencies that will try to understand the victims, solve the problems, and promote workable compromises? Adversary rhetoric and group conflict have reached a point in our time when uncontrolled advocacy is creating substantial fear and anxiety in society at large. The nightly cancer scares on television news programs, promoted by the publicity releases of politicians and environmental groups, are probably quite effective in securing the attention of mass audiences, but they are also very dangerous business. Undisciplined advocacy can easily create mobs when there is so much urban stress and when the power of emotional issues can be so easily amplified by the hoopla of the mass media. We saw the danger signs during the rising drama of the Watergate impeachment proceeding when paranoia and hatred were almost uncontrolled in Washington and a national catastrophe was averted only because of the strength of our courts.

The courts, however, are not enough. They are built upon a legal framework stressing adversary conflict whereas the nation's need for reason and self-understanding requires an equally powerful commitment from institutions committed to healing and harmony. Consider the harm that unbridled advocacy has brought to the practice of medi-

cine, with today's proliferation of malpractice lawsuits as
a way of seeking compensation for real and imagined medical injuries if you wish to grasp my essential meaning.

The principal danger of the growing adversary character of American public life, as I have tried to argue, lies in
the creation of growing numbers of existential victims ripe
for manipulation by demagogues and revolutionaries. It
can easily lead to further weakening of a society already
burdened with existential stresses. A second major concern
is the demonstrated effectiveness of newly devised adversary
tactics in achieving remarkable benefits for a limited number of constituencies. The danger is that many other groups
in society will be attracted by such successes, and move
rapidly into the whirlpool of warring constituencies.

Institutions such as the University or the church, and
professions such as medicine and teaching were never designed for combat. They have demeaned themselves whenever they have lost sight of their philosophical underpinnings. Gandhi was able to galvanize India via the exercise
of a simple but extraordinary religious force, accomplishing
political objectives without engaging overtly in political
struggle. Martin Luther King found the same resonant
chord in the early days of the American civil rights movement.

Some in this audience may have visited the Basilica of
Our Lady of Guadalupe in Mexico City. I wonder if you
were struck as I was by the sheer power of faith in the
thousands, coming from all over Mexico day after day,
crawling on their knees across that huge plaza, to present
themselves and their babies to the brown-skinned Virgin
who protects them. There is nothing like it in Rome, and
nothing like it in Washington. It is something beyond this
world.

I can offer no simple formula for achieving such moral
power. Finding it in any particular set of circumstances is
the heart of the matter. If I were truly capable and truly
wise, I would long ago have fashioned Columbia University

into a more effective institution for leading the nation at a time when so much leadership seems based upon energizing despair, and when rational but difficult courses of action are attacked by innumerable coalitions of narrow, self-serving interests. I offer only an attempt to characterize and identify the worrisome adversary directions of our time and then to counsel you that neither Columbia nor the judiciary will ever be very credible as leaders of a troubled society if we limit our concerns to self-serving advocacy or existential despair.

Both of us possess a very special and very precious moral eminence. We must use that eminence to guide others wisely, to analyze problems, suggest compromises, and to propose solutions. As an alternative to the protesters and the victims, we and other constructive forces in society must exercise our special capacity for healing wounds and solving problems. Our form of leadership must be fundamentally different from that sought via the rhetoric of social protest. We must use the credibility and eminence deriving from our position apart from meaner forms of political strife in order to diminish conflict not to attempt to profit from it. We in the academic world must above all else stand for reason and humanity in finding solutions to the dilemma posed by the goal of a humane society that does not create numberless existential victims, a dilemma that now obsesses most of western culture. You in the judiciary must be committed not just to the rule of law, but also the resolution of many forms of human conflict outside the courts by non-adversary methods based on the creation of intergroup harmony.

Just as universities can no longer pretend to stand apart from the society that sustains them but must involve themselves directly in the analysis and solution of society's problems, the judiciary must draw back from efforts to resolve many forms of human conflict within the adversary framework which they administer.

We must proceed not in the fashion of the protesters

of the 1960's but more in the manner pioneered by Jesus,
Gandhi and Martin Luther King. Together we must try
to move from today's environment, replete with anxiety,
struggle and existential victimization to a new vision of
America more closely attuned to the idealism of our forefathers.

COMMITMENT TO SCHOLARSHIP
AND RESEARCH [1]

WILLIAM G. BOWEN [2]

Dr. William G. Bowen, president of Princeton University, recently described "the proper function" of associations such as the American Council on Education and Association of American Universities as follows:

> To educate Congress and the wider public to the nature and purposes of higher education. And to help enhance understanding. Much hard work has to be done; there are no magical levers to be pulled. It calls for patient and persistent efforts to be helpful and available to talk with Congressmen and their staffs to provide information and answer questions (*Change,* April 1979, p. 32).

As immediate past chairman of ACE and a member of the board of AAU and as a recognized authority in the field of education-government relations, Bowen is well qualified to be a spokesman who "provides information and answers questions" on academic matters at the highest levels.

The president of Princeton fulfilled this role in an address at a luncheon at the Princeton Club of Washington, which met at the Rayburn House Office Building, March 7, 1979. The meeting was in honor of Princetonians who serve in Congress and in other governmental agencies. Included in this group are five senators, nine representatives, and about sixty persons who serve on congressional staffs, joint committees, and agencies.

The total number of Princetonians working in the federal government in Washington is approximately 300. Dr. Bowen was aware of the fact that this audience was in a position to wield considerable influence in governmental matters. Throughout his low-key speech, he emphasized the importance of university scholarship and research to our nation's future, to our international relations, and to our individual lives. He reviewed the contribu-

---

[1] Delivered at a luncheon in honor of Princetonians in Congress and on Capitol Hill, meeting in Room B338–340 Rayburn Office Building, Washington, D.C., March 7, 1979. Quoted by permission. Title supplied by editor.

[2] For biographical note, see Appendix.

tions made to American industry, the economy in general, and national security, but at the same time, indicated that scholarship and research are hampered by insufficient federal funds and burdensome federal regulations. The speech is a good example of persuasion by implication.

In Alec Leitch's *Princeton Companion* published last fall [1978], the legacy to the university from Woodrow Wilson (of this year's centennial Class of 1879) is described as "a vision of an institution dedicated both to things of the mind and the nation's service. . . ."

That continues to be our vision, and we fulfill it in essential ways through our commitment to scholarship and research of the highest quality. This will be the theme of my annual report to the university community later this spring, and I would like to take advantage of this very special gathering here in Washington to discuss with you what I believe are—and should be—widely shared convictions and concerns in this area.

As Jim Leach [Republican, Iowa] emphasized on the floor of the House last year, and as President Carter stated in his recent budget message, scholarship and research constitute an essential investment in the nation's future. They yield insights and discoveries that increase productivity, that enhance the competitive position of American industry, and that can serve to improve standards of living all over the world. While precise calculations of economic effects are not possible, careful studies suggest that advances in knowledge have accounted for roughly one quarter to one third of the increase in national income in the United States since 1929.

As is evident in the sciences and engineering, but is no less true in other branches of knowledge which help us to understand other peoples and societies, scholarship and research also contribute importantly to national security and improved international relations. They are essential as well to the very concept of freedom. I do not believe I exaggerate when I say that all the freedoms of our society depend in significant degree on the critical exercise of scholarship and research, unfettered by any ideological or political harness and uncompromising in the pursuit of truth.

Finally, scholarship and research matter greatly for more intangible reasons that have to do with our zest for learning, and with the hopes, fears, and spiritual concerns that drive us. Any literate society, interested in human values, needs its poets and philosophers, its art historians and its scholars of religion, no less than its physicists, mathematicians, and engineers. All are necessary for our health and vitality—and perhaps even for our individual and collective sanity. (Please note that at this point in time I did not think it appropriate to mention economists!)

Fortunately, there is today in the United States an enviable capacity for outstanding accomplishments in many disciplines—much of it, especially in scientific fields, developed since World War II. According to figures compiled by the National Science Foundation, for example, of 492 major technological innovations in the period 1953 to 1973, 65 percent resulted from work in the United States. And 50 percent of the Nobel Prizes in science awarded since the war have gone to Americans, as opposed to only 20 percent up to that time.

As we think about the origins of this capacity to generate new ideas, we need to remember Francis Bacon's injunction of three and a half centuries ago that we must "from experience of every kind first endeavor to discover true causes and axioms; and seek for experiments of Light, not for experiments of Fruit. For axioms, rightly discovered and established, supply practice with its instruments not one by one, but in clusters, and draw after them trains and troops of works."

While the task of finding applications of new knowledge is obviously of enormous importance, the applications and the technologies of any given age depend critically on the basic research of earlier times, generally conducted by people interested in understanding the fundamental "axioms" of their fields without the deliberate intention of solving a practical problem or achieving a specific utilitarian end.

I realize that basic research frequently is criticized—and sometimes even ridiculed—by those who question its significance and who seek assurances of more or less immediate payoffs. In assessing such views, we do well to recall that the most important medical advances of this century are rooted in basic research that included no hint whatsoever of such applications as the development of antibiotics, that one of the most important "practical" discoveries of all time (hybrid corn) owes much to a one-time Princeton professor, George Shull, who was equally fascinated by his studies of the evening primrose, and that the modern science of genetics received more than a small push forward as a result of a study by Gregor Mendel that could well have been titled "How to Segregate Round from Wrinkled Peas" —a surefire candidate for a "Golden Fleece" award in its time.

It certainly is true that scholarship and research, and even basic research, are conducted in places other than universities, but universities offer special advantages, and evidence suggests that the university environment has proven to be exceptionally conducive to major advances in knowledge.

To cite just one set of findings: When the National Science Foundation recently compiled a list of 85 significant advances over the past 20 years in four fields (mathematics, chemistry, astronomy, and the earth sciences), university scientists were found to have been responsible for more than 70 percent of them. (I might note that a tabulation of where the university scientists received their highest degrees showed that, as small as it is, Princeton ranked fifth, and was one of only four universities—with Harvard, the University of California at Berkeley, and Columbia—to have educated at least one person in each of the four fields. A tabulation of where the work was done showed that Princeton ranked second, behind only the California Institute of Technology.)

There are, I believe, several characteristics of universities which account in large measure for this record of accomplishment. First, universities are committed to the twin concepts of academic freedom and the pursuit of the most fundamental questions, however unsettling or controversial they may be. Moreover, the university environment tends to encourage independent thinking, comprised as it is of individuals who are charged with a particular responsibility to think for themselves, to challenge each other as well as orthodoxies old and new, and to feel no obligation to follow anyone else's sense of the right way to attack a particular problem.

Another characteristic of universities is that they encompass work in a great variety of disciplines. Thus it is possible—though no one should claim that it happens always or necessarily—for faculty members in various fields to "kibitz" on the work of colleagues in other fields, thereby providing fresh perspectives and some hope of avoiding overly narrow approaches to fundamental problems. The relatively small size and the cohesiveness of Princeton offer special opportunities in this regard, and the cross-departmental programs we have established in such areas as energy and environmental studies, East Asian and Near Eastern studies, and economic development and modernization represent efforts to take advantage of this characteristic.

Finally, universities are "special" because of the interrelationship between research and teaching which is as important as it is evident. The involvement of graduate students in advanced research—and frequently at Princeton of undergraduates as well—not only provides exceptional opportunities to prepare the next generation of scholars, but benefits the scholarship and research of this generation by subjecting it to new sources of criticism. Almost every faculty member on our campus, I suspect, can cite examples where students have asked a question or made a suggestion that opened a promising new line of inquiry, clarified a puzzle, or called into question a convention that ultimately proved to be deficient.

What this means, in part, is that the investment in university research produces a double benefit: Not only is the research accomplished in an unusually conducive environment, but those who will be the research leaders of the next generation are instructed and encouraged at the same time.

This relationship between scholarship and research, on the one hand, and teaching, on the other, was discussed in a memorable Baccalaureate address given in 1975 by Gregory Vlastos, at that time the distinguished chairman of our Philosophy Department, when he identified four processes necessary to advance and disseminate knowledge: (1) the discovery of new ideas and new forms; (2) the critical scrutiny of these innovations; (3) the assimilation of these very new results with the vast inheritance of previously discovered knowledge; and (4) the transmission of appropriate portions of this aggregate to succeeding generations of incoming students. "The excellences at the two extremes—of research and teaching," he went on to say, "have essential bonds with what comes in between—with criticism and erudition: without excellence in each of these the creator's work would be wild and the teacher's shallow."

As we look to the future of scholarship and research, we need to bear in mind that, as always, it is the quality of the people involved that matters most—our principal task is educating, recruiting, and motivating those rare individuals who are genuinely creative as well as committed to the hard work that is indispensable to first-rate scholarship and research. Unhappily, however, even the best people generally require at least some support. I am not convinced that the hair shirt will attract the best people to theology or poetry, never mind to Chinese politics or Plasma Physics. To be sure, pain can lead to creativity—but these days it would be more than just fashionably outrageous to argue the case for poverty as a stimulus to good work; it would be extraordinarily foolish and extraordinarily dangerous.

In my annual report, I shall describe in some detail the decrease in the real value of federal support for scholarship and research that has been a fact of the last decade at the major research universities. From a national standpoint, suffice it to say that the federal government supports about two-thirds of the nation's total basic research effort and more than two-thirds of all research and development conducted at colleges and universities. And federal support for basic research, in constant dollars, has declined by roughly five percent over the last decade. Looked at another way, between 1962 and 1975, while the fraction of GNP devoted to research and development in West Germany increased by 80 percent and the comparable fraction in Japan grew by 31 percent, in the United States there was a 15 percent decline.

This is a time, I know, when many of us question the role of government in various areas; I know that I do. But let us make no mistake about the role of government in supporting basic research. It is rooted directly in the character of the activity: basic research is unpredictable, and the benefits it confers take the form of new ideas which no private entity can keep entirely to itself, but which naturally and inevitably "spill over" to the entire society. Accordingly, there is widespread agreement with the proposition that government has a clear responsibility to foster advances in knowledge which are the common property of all. President Carter, his science advisor Frank Press, and others have spoken forcefully of the importance of increasing support for research, and especially basic research, and they have done so at a time of great budgetary stringency. They deserve credit for making this case, and the case they have made deserves the support of all who have a sense of the long-term values at stake.

Beyond the general question of levels of support, I have time today only to mention, almost in passing, five other specific concerns related to the future of scholarship and research—all of them, I think, familiar to you, and all deserving of much more attention than I can give them in this talk.

First, there is the terribly discouraging outlook for young scholars in essentially all fields of knowledge. As is well known, various factors—anticipated declines in enrollment, an unfavorable age distribution of faculties, tight budgets, and legislative pressures for later retirement—have combined to diminish drastically opportunities for new people to be appointed and then advanced. One set of projections done for the American Council on Education illustrates the seriousness of the problem. If certain factors are held constant (student-teacher ratios, fractions of age-groups being educated, etc.), and if all faculty members who do not retire before age 65 were to continue teaching until 70, aggregative statistical projections indicate that on a net basis there would be literally *no* new faculty openings across the country for six consecutive years—from 1983 through 1988. All such projections are of course based on assumptions subject to modification, and I am certain that in fact there will be some openings in many institutions, including Princeton. Still, the national outlook has to be seen as bleak —and not of course just for the individuals concerned, but for the quality of teaching and research, dependent as it is on new people, new ideas, and the continuity of research efforts. We cannot afford to lose a generation.

Second, there is the problem of support for the major tools of scholarship and research—which are very expensive. Special mention has to be made of the major research libraries, critical as they are to scholarship in all fields, and of the costs involved in providing proper equipment and instrumentation in laboratories. What is needed in these areas is both more money and some new organizational arrangements that will facilitate the sharing of costly resources.

Third, there is a danger that the combination of severe budgetary limitations, political pressures to spread the available funds broadly, and worries about "relevance" will strengthen the inclination of both writers of proposals and reviewers of proposals to prefer "safe" projects. Yet, it is often true that the most "unpredictable outcomes" are the most significant. The same NSF study referred to earlier documented the importance of broadly-gauged, flexible research projects. In studying the origins and characteristics of the 85 most significant advances in the four scientific fields over the last 20 years, it was found that only 43 percent of the projects which led to these advances had actually contained, in the funding proposal, a direct reference to the significant outcome; 40 percent of the advances were derived from grants for broadly defined research in the general area; and 17 percent were related neither directly nor generally to the justification used in requesting support.

A fourth concern—and I hate even to mention it because I know everyone in Washington is sick to death of hearing about it—is administrative burdens. Having mentioned it, I'm almost sorry already that I did, because it's become a kind of code phrase, used in some cases to say things I don't want to say but do not have time today to disavow. In any event, it is a fact that, whatever the reasons and justifications, time and personnel available to do research have been reduced by substantially increased administrative demands. As always, what is needed is a balanced perspective, some acceptance by the universities of their own responsibilities to be at least reasonably orderly and businesslike in their procedures, some trust on the part of government, and a renewed determination by all concerned not to let contract administration become an end in itself, independent of, if not destructive of, other goals. When bureaucratic detail and regulatory zeal threaten to crowd out creative effort, there are no winners, and the original purpose of the undertaking is defeated.

Fifth—and this is an enormous subject all its own—in our concern for science, technology, productivity, and all the rest, we dare not lose sight of the importance of those other fields of knowledge which give meaning and direction to our lives. Asymmetries in the support of the sciences and humanities need to be reviewed in the most thoughtful

way—not with an eye to somehow "equalizing" things, an
objective both impossible and undesirable—but with an eye
to recognizing the separate needs and critical contributions
of each set of subjects.

Scholarship and research, and our concerns for their
future, can be thought of in quite practical, utilitarian
terms; and, in one sense, there is nothing wrong with such
a conception since these activities do matter so very importantly to our well-being. But such an orientation is, in my
view, dangerously incomplete.

Ultimately, our commitment to the advancement of
knowledge must be seen at least as much in terms of values
that are more easily felt than entered on any ledger of the
usual kind. For me at least, the importance of our commitment to scholarship and research transcends measurable
needs. It reflects our pressing, irrepressible need as human
beings to seek understanding for its own sake. It is tied in-
extricably to the freedom to think freshly, to see propositions of every kind in ever-changing light. And it celebrates
the special exhilaration that comes from a new idea.

My greatest personal debt to Princeton as a teaching
institution derives from an experience I had as a beginning
graduate student in the fall of 1955. As a student in one of
the last classes in the History of Economic Thought taught
by Professor Jacob Viner, I was given the privilege of
seeing at first hand what constitutes scholarship of a high
order, and how the standards and values of scholarship can
inform work that otherwise might seem routine or pedes-
trian—and, for that matter, can affect the whole of a person's life. I hope that those who were unable to witness
Professor Viner's scholarship, or who do not know the
fruits of it, will nonetheless sense the spirit of what I am
trying to say through the following comment of his:

All that I plead on behalf of scholarship is that, once the
taste for it has been aroused, it gives a sense of largeness even to
one's small quests, and a sense of fullness even to the small answers to problems large or small which it yields, a sense which

can never in any other way be attained, for which no other source of human gratification can, to the addict, be a satisfying substitute, which gains instead of loses in quality and quantity and in pleasure-yielding capacity by being shared with others—and which, unlike golf, improves with age.

QUEST FOR HUMAN DIGNITY

UNIVERSAL DECLARATION OF HUMAN RIGHTS [1]

JIMMY CARTER [2]

The theme of freedom has been centermost in American thought and policy since the days of the colonists. It was expressed in the Declaration of Independence and the Constitution and reaffirmed in the speeches of such great Americans as Daniel Webster, Abraham Lincoln, Woodrow Wilson, and Franklin D. Roosevelt. In his Inaugural Address (January 20, 1977), Jimmy Carter echoed the theme once more, making it a hallmark of our international policy. "Our commitment to human rights must be absolute" and "because we are free, we can never be indifferent to the fate of freedom elsewhere," was his pledge. Many dismissed the Carter statements as inaugural rhetoric, but the President by subsequent actions has shown that this is not the case. Although he has been less vocal about it lately, he has nevertheless persisted in demanding human dignity and freedom in all lands.

The administration took advantage of another occasion to spotlight Carter's human rights policy, on the anniversary of the passage of the United Nations Universal Declaration of Human Rights. At noon, on December 6, 1978, President Carter addressed 200 civil rights and religious leaders, human rights activists, and congressmen in the East Room of the White House. Prior to the President's speech, Secretary of State Cyrus R. Vance, Assistant Secretary of State for Human Rights and Humanitarian Affairs Patricia Derian, National Security Affairs Adviser Zbigniew Brzezinski, and Presidential Assistant Anne Wexler conducted a one-hour briefing on foreign policy.

Then, the President made one of his strongest statements on human rights, saying "human rights is the soul of our foreign policy" and "no force on Earth can separate us from that commitment." Although this sympathic audience responded enthusiastically to the speech, there was an exception. Vernon Bellecourt of the National Council of the American Indian Movement thought it "despicable" to discuss human rights when they were "denied to American Indians."

---

[1] Delivered at 12 noon, December 6, 1978, in the East Room of the White House, Washington, D.C.

[2] For biographical note, see Appendix.

Those interested in other recent statements on the human rights issue should read Daniel P. Moynihan's "Worldwide Amnesty for Political Prisoners (*Representative American Speeches,* 1975–1976, p 65–7), Cyrus R. Vance's "Human Rights and the Foreign Policy" (*Ibid.,* 1976-1977, p 127-38), and Arthur J. Goldberg's "Human Rights and Détente" (*Ibid.,* 1977–1978, p 71–82).

What I have to say today is fundamentally very simple. It's something I've said many times, including my acceptance speech when I was nominated as President and my inaugural speech when I became President. But it cannot be said too often or too firmly nor too strongly.

As long as I am President, the government of the United States will continue throughout the world to enhance human rights. No force on earth can separate us from that commitment.

This week we commemorate the 30th anniversary of the Universal Declaration of Human Rights. We rededicate ourselves—in the words of Eleanor Roosevelt, who was the chairperson of the Human Rights Commission—to the Universal Declaration as, and I quote from her, "a common standard of achievement for all peoples of all nations."

The Universal Declaration and the human rights conventions that derive from it do not describe the world as it is. But these documents are very important, nonetheless. They are a beacon, a guide to a future of personal security, political freedom, and social justice.

For millions of people around the globe that beacon is still quite distant, a glimmer of light on a dark horizon of deprivation and repression. The reports of Amnesty International, the International Commission of Jurists, the International League for Human Rights, and many other nongovernmental human rights organizations amply document the practices and conditions that destroy the lives and the spirit of countless human beings.

Political killings, tortures, arbitrary and prolonged detention without trial or without a charge, these are the cruelest and the ugliest of human rights violations. Of all human rights, the most basic is to be free of arbitrary violence, whether that violence comes from government, from terrorists, from criminals, or from self-appointed messiahs operating under the cover of politics or religion.

But governments—because of their power, which is so much greater than that of an individual—have a special responsibility. The first duty of a government is to protect its own citizens, and when government itself becomes the perpetrator of arbitrary violence against its citizens, it undermines its own legitimacy.

There are other violations of the body and the spirit which are especially destructive of human life. Hunger, disease, poverty, are enemies of human potential which are as relentless as any repressive government.

The American people want the actions of their government, our government, both to reduce human suffering and to increase human freedom. That's why—with the help and encouragement of many of you in this room—I have sought to rekindle the beacon of human rights in American foreign policy. Over the last two years we've tried to express these human concerns as our diplomats practice their craft and as our nation fulfills its own international obligations.

We will speak out when individual rights are violated in other lands. The Universal Declaration means that no nation can draw the cloak of sovereignty over torture, disappearances, officially sanctioned bigotry, or the destruction of freedom within its own borders. The message that is being delivered by all our representatives abroad—whether they are from the Department of State or Commerce or Agriculture or Defense or whatever—is that the policies regarding human rights count very much in the character of our own relations with other individual countries.

In distributing the scarce resources of our foreign assistance programs, we will demonstrate that our deepest affinities are with nations which commit themselves to a democratic path to development. Toward regimes which persist in wholesale violations of human rights, we will not hesitate to convey our outrage, nor will we pretend that our relations are unaffected.

In the coming year, I hope that Congress will take a step that has been long overdue for a generation, the ratification of the Convention on the Prevention and Punishment of the Crime of Genocide. As you know, the genocide convention was also adopted by the United Nations General Assembly 30 years ago this week, one day before the adoption of the Universal Declaration. It was the world's affirmation that the lesson of the Holocaust would never be forgotten, but unhappily, genocide is not peculiar to any one historical era.

Eighty-three other nations have ratified the genocide convention. The United States, despite the support of every President since 1948, has not. In international meetings at the United Nations and elsewhere, when I meet with foreign leaders, we are often asked why. We do not have an acceptable answer.

I urge the United States Senate to observe this anniversary in the only appropriate way, by ratifying the genocide convention at the earliest possible date.

This action must be the first step toward the ratification of other human rights instruments, including those I signed a year ago. Many of the religious and human rights groups represented here have undertaken a campaign of public education on behalf of these covenants. I commend and appreciate your efforts.

Refugees are the living, homeless casualties of one very important failure on the part of the world to live by the principles of peace and human rights. To help these refugees is a simple human duty. As Americans, as a people made up largely of the descendants of refugees, we feel that duty with special keenness.

Our country will do its utmost to ease the plight of stranded refugees from Indochina and from Lebanon and of released political prisoners from Cuba and from elsewhere. I hope that we will always stand ready to welcome more than our fair share of those who flee their homelands because of racial, religious, or political oppression.

The effectiveness of our human rights policy is now an established fact. It has contributed to an atmosphere of change—sometimes disturbing—but which has encouraged progress in many ways and in many places. In some countries, political prisoners have been released by the hundreds, even thousands. In others, the brutality of repression has been lessened. In still others there's a movement toward democratic institutions or the rule of law when these movements were not previously detectable.

To those who doubt the wisdom of our dedication, I say this: Ask the victims. Ask the exiles. Ask the governments which continue to practice repression. Whether in Cambodia or Chile, in Uganda or South Africa, in Nicaragua or Ethiopia or the Soviet Union, governments know that we in the United States care. And not a single one of those who is actually taking risks or suffering for human rights has ever asked me to desist in our support of basic human rights. From the prisons, from the camps, from the enforced exiles, we receive one message: Speak up, persevere, let the voice of freedom be heard.

I'm very proud that our nation stands for more than military might or political might. It stands for ideals that have their reflection in the aspirations of peasants in Latin America, workers in Eastern Europe, students in Africa, and farmers in Asia.

We do live in a difficult and complicated world, a world in which peace is literally a matter of survival. Our foreign policy must take this into account. Often, a choice that moves us toward one goal tends to move us further away from another goal. Seldom do circumstances permit me or you to take actions that are wholly satisfactory to everyone.

But I want to stress again that human rights are not peripheral to the foreign policy of the United States. Our human rights policy is not a decoration. It is not something we've adopted to polish up our image abroad or to put a fresh coat of moral paint on the discredited policies of the past. Our pursuit of human rights is part of a broad effort to use our great power and our tremendous influence in the service of creating a better world, a world in which human beings can live in peace, in freedom, and with their basic needs adequately met.

Human rights is the soul of our foreign policy. And I say this with assurance, because human rights is the soul of our sense of nationhood.

For the most part, other nations are held together by common racial or ethnic ancestry, or by a common creed or religion, or by ancient attachments to the land that go back for centuries of time. Some nations are held together by the forces, implied forces of a tyrannical government. We are different from all of those, and I believe that we in our country are more fortunate.

As a people we come from every country and every corner of the earth. We are of many religions and many creeds. We are of every race, every color, every ethnic and cultural background. We are right to be proud of these things and of the richness that lend to the texture of our national life. But they are not the things which unite us as a single people.

What unites us—what makes us Americans—is a common belief in peace, in a free society, and a common devotion to the liberties enshrined in our Constitution. That belief and that devotion are the sources of our sense of national community. Uniquely, ours is a nation founded on an idea of human rights. From our own history we know how powerful that idea can be.

Next week marks another human rights anniversary— Bill of Rights Day. Our nation was "conceived in liberty," in Lincoln's words, but it has taken nearly two centuries for that liberty to approach maturity.

For most of the first half of our history, black Americans were denied even the most basic human rights. For most of the first two-thirds of our history, women were excluded from the political process. Their rights and those of native Americans are still not constitutionally guaranteed and enforced. Even freedom of speech has been threatened periodically throughout our history. Only in the last 10 to 12 years have we achieved what Father Hesburgh has called "the legal abandonment of more than three centuries of apartheid." And the struggle for full human rights for all Americans—black, brown, and white; male and female; rich and poor—is far from over.

To me, as to many of you, these are not abstract matters or ideas. In the rural Georgia country where I grew up, the majority of my own fellow citizens were denied many basic rights—the right to vote, the right to speak freely without fear, the right to equal treatment under the law. I saw at first hand the effects of a system of deprivation of rights. I saw the courage of those who resisted that system. And finally, I saw the cleansing energies that were released when my own region of this country walked out of darkness and into what Hubert Humphrey, in the year of the adoption of the Universal Declaration, called "the bright sunshine of human rights."

The American Bill of Rights is 187 years old, and the struggle to make it a reality has occupied every one of those 187 years. The Universal Declaration of Human Rights is only 30 years old. In the perspective of history, the idea of human rights has only just been broached.

I do not draw this comparison because I want to counsel patience. I draw it because I want to emphasize, in spite of difficulties, steadfastness and commitment.

A hundred and eighty-seven years ago, as far as most Americans were concerned, the Bill of Rights was a bill of promises. There was no guarantee that those promises would ever be fulfilled. We did not realize those promises by waiting for history to take its inevitable course. We realized them because we struggled. We realized them because many sacrificed. We realized them because we persevered.

For millions of people around the world today the Universal Declaration of Human Rights is still only a declaration of hope. Like all of you, I want that hope to be fulfilled. The struggle to fulfill it will last longer than the lifetimes of any of us. Indeed, it will last as long as the lifetime of humanity itself. But we must persevere.

And we must persevere by ensuring that this country of ours, leader in the world, which we love so much, is always in the forefront of those who are struggling for that great hope, the great dream of universal human rights.

"WHEN FREEDOM DIES IN ITS SLEEP" [1]

ROBERT P. GRIFFIN [2]

The trials of three Soviet dissidents, Alexander Ginzburg, Anatoly Shcharansky, and Vibtorus Petkus, stirred outrage, sympathy, and frustration among Americans, and many groups sought to exert pressure on the US government to intervene.

One such group, the National Committee for Human Rights and Fundamental Freedoms, founded in 1975, "works for the release of men and women who are in prison for their beliefs, color, ethnic orgin or religion provided they have not used force nor advocated violence." Its annual conference, called "The Final Act" and held on Saturday, August 19, 1978, had for its primary purpose "to remind everyone in the election year that the human rights provisions of the *Final Act on Security and Cooperation in Europe*, signed in Helsinki, have been systematically violated by the USSR."

Senator Robert P. Griffin (Republican, Michigan) gave the keynote speech at a banquet that concluded a day-long conference. The meeting, held at the Kalamazoo Hilton Inn, attracted about 200 persons from several states. Participating were officers of several nationalist-oriented associations of Baltic and European nations under Russian occupation. At the time of the speech, Senator Griffin was running for re-election (he was defeated) and he was a member of the Senate Foreign Relations Committee. His address, in the mode of a campaign speech, was designed to appeal to his partisan audience. First, he reiterated the numerous Soviet violations of human rights and the Helsinki-Belgrade Accords, indicating that there were only limited improvements resulting from the latter. Then, critical of détente, he called for a consistent foreign policy and a militarily strong America to counteract Soviet aggressions.

Chairman Strautkalns, distinguished guests and friends: Flagrant violations of human rights in Soviet-dominated

[1] Delivered as the keynote address at banquet of the National Committee for Human Rights and Fundamental Freedoms, at Hilton Inn, Kalamazoo, Michigan, August 18, 1978. Title supplied by editor. From the *Congressional Record*, August 25, 1978, p S14575–6.

[2] For biographical note, see Appendix.

countries continue unabated despite the promises given in Helsinki and Belgrade [Conference on Security and Cooperation in Europe]. This is intolerable and we would betray our own heritage as Americans if we were to remain silent in the face of such oppression.

The basic question suggested by the topic of your conference is this: Has the Helsinki-Belgrade experience been a success—or a failure—from a human rights standpoint?

The answer, of course, depends largely upon what one expected to achieve through the European Security Conference mechanism.

Those who really expected "nothing," have not been disappointed.

At the other extreme, it appears that many people thought that once Moscow supposedly had "agreed" in Helsinki to respect human rights, some kind of a major transformation would somehow occur almost immediately in the Soviet Union. By the time Round Two in Belgrade came along, so the theory went, all of the outstanding problems would be resolved. Needless to say, these people, if they have paid attention, have been disappointed.

In all candor, my own expectations were quite limited.

If one really never trusted the Russian leaders to begin with, he would not have expected their agreement to the principles set forth in Basket Three at Helsinki to produce much in the way of concrete results.

After all, if it had been the practice of the Soviets in the past to honor their promises, the whole Helsinki experience would have been unnecessary. History is full of broken Soviet promises to respect human rights. For example:

Stalin's 1936 Constitution of the USSR supposedly "guaranteed" freedom of religious worship, freedom of speech, freedom of the press, freedom of assembly, and a wealth of other "rights." Of course, they never have been respected.

The 1945 Charter of the United Nations—which Moscow signed—contains numerous references to the UN's purpose of "reaffirming faith in fundamental human rights," of respecting "the principle of equal rights and self-determination of peoples," and of "promoting and encouraging respect for human rights and for fundamental freedoms for all." These rights, too, were subscribed to—but then ignored —by the Kremlin.

In December 1948 the Soviets voted in the General Assembly to adopt the United Nations "Universal Declaration of Human Rights." This document guarantees the right to privacy, the right to own property, freedom of speech, assembly, religion and association. It even says that "(t)he will of the people shall be the basis of the authority of government." Again more rights debased by Moscow.

Thus, history indicates that most, if not all, of the human rights to which Moscow pledged itself three years ago in Helsinki were already allegedly "guaranteed" in other documents to which the Soviets had already officially subscribed. Therefore, it would have been naive in the extreme to assume that somehow this time was going to be significantly different—that Soviet liberalization was just around the corner.

Indeed, our reaction to Helsinki reflects, to a certain degree, a fundamental problem this country has had for more than three decades in dealing with the Soviets. Because we desperately want to see things change, too often we pretend to see change—where no change exists.

Tragically, it sometimes seems that the West did not learn much from Yalta.

Just as the realities subsequent to Yalta seemed to catch Roosevelt and Churchill by surprise, those who though they saw a new Soviet Union in the early 1950s had a rude awakening with the October 1956 Soviet invasion of Hungary.

Tomorrow—August 20 [1978]—will mark the tenth anniversary of an event that once again temporarily brought realism to Western perception of Soviet realities. I speak of the invasion of Czechoslovakia.

Not many years ago—when the term détente was in more respectable use—it was popular in some quarters to describe the Soviet Union as a "status quo power," uninterested in foreign adventurism.

Then came Africa—with billions of dollars in Soviet military aid and tens of thousands of Cuban mercenaries.

Today the Russians and their Cuban puppets are involved in no fewer than five wars in Africa—and yet our ambassador to the United Nations assures us that things have never been better.

I don't suggest that it is hopeless even to try to affect Soviet policy. But my point is that we must be realistic.

Indeed, experience has demonstrated that, on occasion, we have had some limited success in bringing about desirable changes in Soviet policy.

In 1962, President John Kennedy's firm stand led to a withdrawal of Russian missiles from Cuba.

In 1972, President Nixon's use of increased force against North Vietnam resulted in Soviet pressure on Hanoi to conclude a peace agreement.

And Western pressure concerning Soviet human rights violations have produced some limited beneficial results.

Nevertheless, we would be naive in the extreme to assume that those limited successes signaled any basic change in Soviet goals or strategy.

In 1920, Lenin wrote that compromise is essential for the eventual success of communism. Lenin told his supporters to fight only when what he called the "correlation of forces," was favorable; and until then to compromise and maneuver as necessary to weaken the enemy and to increase the forces of communism.

In large measure, this strategy has worked for the Communists, and it is still being followed by Moscow. The result has been that whenever the Soviets have perceived that the United States has both superior military strength—and the will to use it if necessary—the Soviets have followed Lenin's advice and have backed down.

Khrushchev withdrew his missiles from Cuba in 1962 not because he changed his mind about their military utility. He withdrew because he became convinced that the United States had both the strength and the will to make the costs of Soviet adventurism greater than the expected benefits.

Thus, common sense—as well as the lessons of history—tell me that the danger of war increases when the United States grows weak—or if the United States is ever perceived by a potential enemy as being weak.

Common sense—as well as the lessons of history—tell me that the prospects for peace are brighter when the United States is strong—strong not only in military power but strong also in terms of patriotism and the will to defend freedom, when necessary.

Unfortunately, the perception of the United States has been suffering under the leadership of the current administration.

It is important to the United States and the free world that the administration get its act together and that various spokesmen for the White House start reading from the same script—at least in foreign affairs.

National unity and resolve are difficult to achieve unless there first is unity within the administration itself. Not only has there been inconsistency between statements made by White House spokesmen, but there has even been inconsistency between statements made by the President from day to day.

For example, on March 17 of this year [1978] President Carter delivered a hard-hitting speech in North Carolina about the need for a strong national defense.

But, just a few days later he turned around and ordered the Navy's shipbuilding program cut in half.

Then, following a vigorous propaganda campaign waged by the Soviet Union, he postponed production of the newly-developed neutron warhead (referred to by some as the

"neutron bomb"), which, if deployed, could help significantly to offset the massive Soviet advantages in tanks and
other conventional forces in Europe.

And these two announcements came after the President
had already cancelled production of the B–1 bomber—a
decision leaving the US dependent upon World War II-
vintage bomber planes, so old that some of our B–52 pilots
are flying the same aircraft that their fathers flew two
decades ago. This, while Moscow moves full-speed ahead
with production of their supersonic BACKFIRE bomber and
with development of a second strategic bomber that, according to intelligence reports, has characteristics strikingly
similar to our B–1.

Problems resulting from conflicting signals from the
President, himself, are further complicated by the varying
positions taken by his senior advisers. For example, on the
issue of Cuban adventurism in Africa, Secretary of State
Vance, National Security Adviser Brzezinski and UN Ambassador Young all have taken different stands.

Despite such shortcomings in our own foreign policy,
there have been a few positive signs as a consequence of the
Helsinki-Belgrade experience.

In the Soviet Union, I understand that the cost of an
exit visa has declined by half since Helsinki; and on the
eve of Belgrade, Jewish emigration increased by more than
60 percent. Last year in the Ukraine, limited quantities of
some 32 Western newspapers became available for the first
time.

In Hungary, the last three years has brought a notice-
able increase in religious freedom. Both evangelist Billy
Graham and the president of the National Council of
Catholic Bishops made week-long visits to Hungary.

In Poland, authorities last year announced a general
amnesty for some 10,000 persons, and at the time of Belgrade began greater cooperation on family reunification
cases presented by the US Embassy.

In Bulgaria, prospects for family reunification also have

improved and Western Literature—including newspapers and American novels—have become available.

In Czechoslovakia, there has been a noticeable improvement in emigration policy, and in June of last year the government proclaimed an amnesty for Czechs who fled during the Soviet invasion ten years ago.

Finally, in Romania, two general amnesty orders last year brought the release of 30,000 prisoners; and emigration to the United States has increased 21 percent.

But another important benefit of the Helsinki-Belgrade process has been the opportunity it has provided for representatives of this country to raise the issues of human rights with the Soviet Union and Eastern European nations.

Last November, for example, my friend and colleague Senator Dole delivered a speech stressing the fact that the United States has never recognized the Soviet incorporation of Lithuania, Latvia and Estonia. And that must continue to be our policy.

At first the Russians tried to avoid the whole issue of human rights—arguing that raising such questions amounted to an interference in the internal affairs of another State, which is prohibited by the Final Act of Helsinki.

This reasoning was rejected. Soon, the Soviets tried to counterattack by charging "racism" and human rights violations by the US and other Western countries. In so doing, however, they implicitly acknowledged, at least, that human rights are a legitimate and fundamental issue of East-West relations.

Even if the Helsinki-Belgrade process has accomplished nothing else, this recognition that human rights are an integral part of détente can be viewed as a significant achievement.

The Communists have heard the criticism, and it has had some effect.

But, of course, there is no basis or reason for a great deal of optimism. It's true that the 1975 Helsinki Conference led to the establishment of "Helsinki Watch" groups in Moscow and in other Soviet dominated areas—and that is good. But it is also true that more than 30 percent of the members of those groups are now in confinement, and others have been sent into foreign exile.

It is true that in some instances emigration figures increased immediately prior to the Belgrade conference. But it is also true that after Belgrade, people like Petkus, Rostropovich, Ginzburg and Shcharansky have received harsh sentences for advocating respect for human rights.

This brings us to the real question: What should be our policy in seeking to promote an improvement in human rights policies behind the Iron Curtain:

I suggest that three elements are necessary for a successful policy in this regard:

First of all, our commitment to the cause of human rights must be a real commitment, and not be limited to the kind of selective moral outrage that has characterized so much of the rhetoric in recent months. For example, is criticism by this administration of human rights practices in Rhodesia and South Africa to be judged when the administration ignores serious human rights violations in the so-called "front line" African states of Tanzania, Mozambique and Angola? Similarly, it seems a bit strange to hear some spokesmen condemn violations in Chile, South Korea and the Philippines and then express only kind words for the Communist regimes in Cuba and Indochina. If our efforts on behalf of international human rights are to be productive, they must not be perceived simply as politically expedient posturing.

Second, we must project a policy of strength as well as consistency in our dealings with other nations. This means we must have military and economic capabilities that are second to none, and we must make clear that we do have the will to use that strength if necessary.

The third requirement for a successful human rights policy vis à vis the Soviet Union must be the creative and consistent use of incentives. We need to reinforce responsible behavior and punish irresponsible behavior—the old "carrot-and-stick" approach. Earlier this month Ray Moseley—formerly European news editor for United Press International and one of the reporters who covered the 1975 Helsinki conference—wrote in the Chicago *Tribune:*

> If the West continues to make the Soviets pay a price for their unwillingness to abide by the rules of civilized conduct, then the Helsinki accords may be viewed in the Kremlin leadership for years to come as one of Leonid Brezhnev's greatest blunders.

I agree—and it is up to the United States to hold Mr. Brezhnev's feet to the fire whenever possible.

In two years the European Security Conference will convene again—in Madrid.

Madrid will provide yet another opportunity to call world attention to continuing Soviet violations of human rights.

But we must not wait until Madrid.

Although it's hardly likely to produce a radical transformation of the Soviet society, events of the recent past have shown that international protest—public and private—does have some effect.

And those of us gathered here tonight must rededicate ourselves to a continuing effort to expose human rights abuses. We must never for a moment let the world forget what is happening. . . . We must never let the Soviet authorities forget that the world is watching.

In concluding many of the speeches I deliver, particularly when I'm speaking before young people, I often express a thought that is not new—but it is a thought that can bear a good deal of repetition. It goes like this:

In the long course of history, freedom has died in various ways. Freedom has died on the battlefield—freedom has died because of ignorance and greed.

But let me suggest that the most ignominious death of all is when freedom dies in its sleep.

I commend you for your efforts to retrieve freedom where it has been lost. May you also be vigilant in making sure that the freedom we enjoy here in America does not die in its sleep.

PRIVACY ON THE ROPES [1]

CHARLES M. MATHIAS JR. [2]

"Each time we give up a bit of information about ourselves
to the government, we give up some of our freedom. . . . When
the government knows all our secrets we stand naked before official power," observed Sam J. Ervin, former senator from North
Carolina (Democrat). But other sources besides government may
store sundry amounts of information about the citizen. In a message to Congress (April 2, 1979) President Carter lamented, "We
confront threats to privacy undreamed of 200 years ago. . . .
Personal information on millions of Americans is being flashed
across the nation from computer to computer" (*Congressional
Record,* April 2, 1979, p S 3771). Today data may come from
businesses, medical agencies, banks, credit bureaus, and law enforcement divisions. Recent decisions of the Supreme Court make
it easier for snoopers to get guarded secrets. Indeed the citizen
does "stand naked" before inquirers and inquisitors and may
become defenseless against those who wish to deny privileges or
exert pressure.

Much concerned about the problem of privacy, Senator
Charles M. Mathias, Jr. addressed the Law Forum of the Law
School, University of Minnesota, Minneapolis, at noon, on Octo-
ber 20, 1978. His audience was composed of about 300 law stu-
dents, faculty members, and citizens from the area. The Minnesota
Law Forum, like the *Law Review,* is a student activity. In fact
the Senator was invited to speak and was introduced by Tom
McDonald, a senior law student.

Gearing his talk to law students, Senator Mathias discussed
those Supreme Court cases—*United States* v *Miller* and *Zurcher* v
Stanford Daily—in which he believes the right to privacy and the
freedom from unlawful searches were set back. However, he points
out that it is now possible to legislate in five specific areas in
order to offset those Court decisions.

Four years ago one of the great connoisseurs of the
Fourth Amendment—[Professor] Anthony G. Amsterdam

---

[1] Delivered at the Law Forum, University of Minnesota, Law School at
noon, October 20, 1978. Quoted by permission.
[2] For biographical note, see Appendix.

[Stanford Law School]—gave a series of lectures here at the University of Minnesota Law School that have since become classics.

Professor Amsterdam, who was guest speaker in your Oliver Wendell Holmes Lecture Series, gave his talks a deceptively modest title. He called them: "Perspectives on the Fourth Amendment." But they were much more than that. They were a definitive examination of the law of "search and seizure" and of our constitutional right to privacy and its uneasy history in the courts.

It would be impossible to improve on those lectures. And I wouldn't presume to try. But, as is the way with Fourth Amendment law, the last word is never spoken and today new threats to privacy loom on our horizon. New court decisions alter earlier perspectives and there is still much to be said.

Privacy—the right to be let alone—is perhaps the most fragile and elusive guarantee in the Constitution. Its roots are in Seventeenth and Eighteenth Century English law, in the idea of the sanctity of the home and private papers. It is a notion that stirred up hot dispute in the years leading up to the American Revolution. And it is a notion that stirs up hot dispute to this day.

After the Founding Fathers added the Bill of Rights to the Constitution, it seemed that the old disputes over personal freedom would at last be put to rest. With the passage of the Bill of Rights, every American had, in the Fourth Amendment, the explicit guarantee that he would be free from arbitrary invasion of his home and that his papers were inviolable.

But, as Thomas Jefferson predicted, "the natural process of things is for liberty to yield and government to gain ground." And so, it has constantly been necessary to curb the impulses of those in power to infringe these rights.

Despite the careful draftmanship and the clear intent of the authors of the Bill of Rights, the right to privacy has had an uneasy history. It has been tested, challenged and litigated constantly. It has been misunderstood and misinterpreted. It has been abused. As the late Justice Felix Frankfurter noted: " (t) he course of true law pertaining to searches and seizures . . . has not . . . run smooth."

In his lectures here, Professor Amsterdam expressed his concern about the "lack of clarity and consistency" in the United States Supreme Court's Fourth Amendment decisions. But he also offered a thoughtful and not unsympathetic analysis of what the Court is up against in trying to construct a decisional framework for applying the Fourth Amendment.

One of the important points he makes is that "the Justices of the Supreme Court, unlike their critics, bear the responsibility of decision," and that, "people who bear that responsibility soon learn that the welter of life is constantly churning up situations in which the application of clear and consistent theories would produce unacceptable results."

I think the point is well-taken. The Court's task is undoubtedly a difficult one. It is wishful thinking to expect the Court always to speak precisely and consistently. But, having said that, I must add that I think the Court could be doing very much better than it is.

No single constitutional provision has occasioned so many reversals of precedent and inconsistent opinions as the Fourth Amendment. And, in the years since Professor Amsterdam spoke here, the situation has gone from bad to worse. The Court has not come any closer to offering a common thread to lead us through the labyrinth of its privacy decisions. Worse still, it has laid down new decisions that provide far less privacy protection than Americans have every right to expect.

As a result, today privacy stands in danger of being overwhelmed.

The incredible technological advances of the twentieth century have transformed both the nature of privacy and the nature of the threats to privacy. Business, commerce, and government now hum to computer rhythms. The bank, credit, medical, and business records of almost all of us are stored away in some electronic memory.

Computers don't discard information, unless they are ordered to. They don't forget it. They amass it. They retain it. And they spew it forth indiscriminately at the touch of a button. Any sort of information, in any quantity, can be flashed from city to city, and from country to country, without the subject knowing anything about it.

Last year I had a personal experience with this. As I entered the office of a government official in Mexico City, he was just turning off his computer screen. He greeted me with a broad smile and, gesturing toward the screen, said, "Ah, Senator Mathias, I have just been learning about you."

To this day, I have no idea what he was learning about me or where the information came from. He may just have been reading my official biography from the *Congressional Directory*. But, for all I know, he was scanning my bank balance and analyzing my credit profile. In any case, the incident brought home to me just how little control we, who live in the computer age, really have over the facts of our lives and over who has access to these facts.

Technological advances have astronomically multiplied the opportunities for intrusions on our privacy.

This situation is dangerous. And its dangers are accentuated by the continuing dispute over whether or not the privacy protections in the Bill of Rights apply to the intrusions worked by electronic technologies. I believe they do. But, constrained too often by a literal, rather than liberal, reading of the Fourth Amendment, the United States Supreme Court has experienced great difficulty in extending the protection against "unreasonable searches and seizures" to the types of intrusions made possible by the electronic wizardry of the twentieth century.

Obviously, the authors of the Constitution could not foresee the electronic age. They could not foresee telephones, wiretaps, bugging devices, laser beams, computers, and data banks. But, "because the Framers of the federal

Constitution were scrupulous to say no more than necessary," as historian Daniel Boorstin points out, "they provided a document uncannily open to the future."

Unfortunately, however, two years ago the present Supreme Court slammed the door on the future in *United States* v. *Miller,* when it ruled that a citizen's bank records are not his private papers and thus are not protected by the Fourth Amendment. As far as the Court is concerned the bank owns your bank records and you're not even entitled to notice before government agents inspect these records.

It is inconceivable to me that in 1976 the Court would read the Fourth Amendment to exclude financial records from its purview, given the economic facts that govern all our lives. But in *Miller* that's just what the Court did.

To get an idea of how serious a threat the *Miller* decision poses to your privacy you need only consider what's in your bank records. A bank record is not just a collection of miscellaneous, anonymous scraps of paper. It is raw material for a collage that, if pieced together, will reveal not only your income and net worth, but your politics, what you read, what you owe, what you buy, the charities you support, the causes you oppose, where you take your vacations, what and how much you eat and drink, and, even what your allergies are. The very richness of the records almost guarantees that, lacking proper judicial safeguards, they will be abused by those who do not scruple about an individual's privacy.

And, remember, *Miller's* ramifications are not limited to bank records. Potentially they extend to the myriad private records we all necessarily entrust to third parties.

Since *Miller,* the only safe way to insure our personal privacy is to adapt our lifestyles to fit in with the Court's curious view of the Fourth Amendment: tear up our bank books, our checks and credit cards, turn back the clock and go back to the good days. Hide our money in our mattresses and do business cash and carry.

But, hold on. Late last term, the Court sent us a signal that even the mattresses of law-abiding Americans may not be safe.

In *Zurcher* v *Stanford Daily* the Supreme Court held that warrants may issue for the search of premises owned or occupied by a person not suspected of criminal activity. So now, the police may obtain warrants to search your office, home or even your mattress, if they have reason to believe that they'll find contraband, instrumentalities, fruits or evidence of a crime. They can do this even though you are innocent of any wrong-doing and when you don't even know that the material is of interest to the police.

That's just what happened in *Zurcher*.

Local police ransacked the Stanford University newspaper offices in an effort to obtain photographs of a campus demonstration, in which nine police officers were injured. The warrant contained no allegation that the staff of the newspaper was involved in the allegedly illegal acts.

The Court's ruling in *Zurcher* came as a shock. In the words of the New York *Times,* it struck "a double blow at individual privacy and press freedom."

I think the American people have every right to believe that, barring absolutely extraordinary circumstances, warrants can not be used to search the homes and offices of non-suspects. They have the right to expect that surprise searches of non-suspects are the exception not the norm; and, that ordinarily third parties would have an opportunity to press their objections to the government's request in court. That opportunity, incidentally would have existed if the Supreme Court in *Zurcher* had adopted the lower court's decision that a subpoena, not a warrant, should normally be used in non-suspect cases.

Regrettably, the high court saw things differently on all scores and disappointed the reasonable expectations of millions of Americans.

It is not hard to see where the Court went wrong in this. Conditioned by Fourth Amendment cases which pitted law enforcement interests against those of criminal suspects, the majority failed to consider properly whether the traditional Fourth Amendment test regarding the issuing of a search warrant—whether sufficient cause existed to believe the material was in a given location—was equally applicable to non-suspect cases. The Court failed to pay proper attention to the important privacy interests inherent in such situations when it merely stated that " (the) Fourth Amendment itself struck the balance between privacy and public need, and there is no occasion or justification for a court to revise the Amendment and strike a new balance by denying a search warrant in the circumstances present here."

I believe the Court's position runs counter to the intent of the authors of the Bill of Rights. It seems to me that they regarded the warrant clause of the Fourth Amendment as an exception to the privacy protections afforded Americans and that they intended it to cover only those instances where criminal suspects are reasonably believed to be in possession of material relevant to a criminal investigation.

The ramifications of the Court's opinion are obvious. Just think back to Watergate. How likely is it that "Deep Throat," the Washington *Post's* anonymous Watergate informant, would have blown the whistle, if the police then had had the authority to obtain a warrant to search the offices of the Washington *Post?* How likely do you think it is that "Deep Throat" would have run the risk of having his identity disclosed to those rogue elephants in the White House that were seriously proposing such things as firebombing the Brookings Institution? I just don't think "Deep Throat" would have let out a gurgle, if there had been a chance of them finding out who he was.

And the ramifications of the *Zurcher* case don't stop with the press. It also raises the specter of police entering your home in search of evidence about a third party and it provides a means for government agents to breach the confidential relationships between doctor and patient, lawyer and client, and priest and penitent.

If this sounds far-fetched, let me remind you of another incident they had at Stanford just five years ago. Then, the police were investigating a sex offense and wanted to examine the psychiatric records of the victim, who had sought help after the offense had been committed. The police had no reason to believe that the psychiatrist would disregard a subpoena or destroy evidence. Nonetheless, they obtained a warrant to search the files of the Stanford psychiatric clinic, where the victim had been treated. And, in the process of an unsuccessful effort to locate the records, they rifled all the patients' files of the clinic, seeing at least the names of each person who had sought help there. And, of course, knocking the privileged relationship into a cocked hat.

This incident was raised by counsel for respondent in the *Zurcher* case.

Justice Stevens noted in his dissent that the problem isn't just that the police can get into private files; but also what they can lawfully seize when they open them.

This would have been less of a problem before 1967 when the Court struck down the so-called "mere evidence" rule. As we all learned in our criminal procedure classes, under that rule the Court drew a distinction between materials which could be searched and seized, such as contraband, and fruits or instrumentalities of crime, and materials which could not, such as one's private papers.

When the Court abandoned the "mere evidence" rule in *Warden* v *Hayden,* it faced a new and formidable task. It would have to devise new constraints on the scope of permissible searches to insure personal privacy would not be swallowed up.

As Justice Stevens noted, *Zurcher* was "the first time that the Court had an opportunity to consider the kind of showing necessary to justify the vastly expanded degree of intrusion upon privacy that is authorized by the opinion in *Warden* v *Hayden.*"

But the Court fell down on the job. Since *Zurcher,* not

only can a warrant now issue for the search of the home or
office of a law-abiding citizen, but any material that is considered relevant to a criminal investigation is fair game,
even possibly a person's private papers.

Zurcher and *Miller* were the one-two punch to our rights
to privacy and some of us are still reeling with disbelief.
But one thing is clear. When the Court falters as guardian
angel of our right to privacy and disappoints the reasonable
expectations of the American people, then Congress must
assume the responsibility to redress the balance. And, I'm
happy to say we are.

For several years now we have been considering proposals to insure the privacy of financial records from arbitrary government inspection. One of the earliest of these—
my Bill of Rights Procedures Act, S. 3440—was introduced
on May 2, 1974. I have been pushing for legislation in this
critical area ever since. S. 14, which I introduced on the
first day of the 95th Congress, is an updated version of the
Bill of Rights Procedures Act. S. 14 deals with the privacy
of bank records and of records held by credit card companies as well.

Last week the Congress passed legislation that estab-
lishes procedural safeguards controlling government access
to bank and credit card company records. It provides as a
matter of federal statutory law that a depositor has a privacy interest in these records and that he can generally
assert that interest when challenging a request for inspection.

It does not accomplish all the objectives of the Bill of
Rights Procedures Act but, it is an important first step.

Equally important, Congress has not ignored the privacy
implications of *Zurcher*. In his opinion for the majority,
Justice White noted that "the Fourth Amendment does not
prevent or advise against legislative or executive efforts to
establish nonconstitutional protection against possible
abuses of the warrant procedure."

That invitation was irresistible. Already over a dozen

bills have been introduced in the Congress aimed at modi-
fying or overcoming the effects of *Zurcher*.

These bills would generally limit searches of non-suspects to instances where there is reason to believe that the
evidence sought will be destroyed or concealed. They
adopted the conclusion of the district court in *Zurcher* that
a subpoena should always be preferred to a search warrant
in non-suspect cases since "a subpoena is much less intrusive than a warrant" and because there "is no opportunity
to challenge the search warrant prior to the intrusion,
whereas one can always move to quash the subpoena before
producing the sought after materials."

The prompt Congressional response to *Zurcher* is certainly welcome. But, the challenge of the task before us is
difficult and complex. When Congress takes up *Zurcher*
proposals again next year, it will have some tough decisions
to make:

Is *Zurcher* amenable to legislative reversal?

Should the legislation cover all third party searches?
or as some have argued,

Should its protections be confined to the press?

Should the proposals cover state and federal officials
alike? And,

Does Congress have the constitutional authority to
reach all state and federal third party searches?

The 96th Congress must act promptly to address the
remaining questions and I am confident that it will. Congress must strike its own double blow in favor of privacy
by passing additional legislation to offset totally *Miller* and
Zurcher.

I'm afraid I've taken too much time and repeated too

much that you already know. But, where the right to privacy is concerned, it is almost impossible to talk too long, too often, or too loudly. For these are the freedoms no despotism can accommodate. They are the rights no free society can be without.

GOVERNMENTAL REFORM

HOW LONG CAN WE COPE? [1]

WARREN E. BURGER [2]

On September 21, 1978, Warren E. Burger, Chief Justice of the United States, delivered the opening address to the National Archives Conference on the Law and American Society: his speech was entitled "New Historical Perspectives and Resources." Meeting in the theater of the National Archives Building in Washington, D.C., the seminar on legal history attracted legal historians, lawyers, political scientists, archivists, and a few members of the press. This occasion was one in a series of seminars held by the National Archives on subjects of mutual interest to those in the scholarly and professional communities who use archives.

During his tenure as Chief Justice (appointed in 1969 by President Nixon), Warren Burger has frequently advocated reform of the judicial process, the courts, the training of trial lawyers, penal and correctional institutions. On this occasion he found the inspiration for his speech in the coming bicentennial (1987-1989) of the writing and ratification of the Constitution. He proposes that "a significant celebration of the creation of our constitutional system" would be "to reexamine each of the three major articles [I, II, III] of our organic law and compare the functions as they have been performed in recent times with the functions contemplated in 1787 by the men at Philadelphia."

With the prestige of his great office behind him, the Chief Justice provides important leadership in pointing the way to reform and change. His suggestions were meant to be neither challenging nor critical of the three branches of government, but a celebration of the tremendous growth and durability of our government under our 200-year-old Constitution. In this speech he is most skillful in assembling pertinent data to give historical perspective to his point of view and to enlighten and encourage his listeners.

It may seem premature to be thinking about the next significant bicentennial celebration in our national life, but

[1] Delivered to Conference on the Law and American Society, at the National Archives, Washington, D.C., at 10:15 A.M., September 21, 1978.
[2] For biographical note, see Appendix.

our experience with the bicentennial of 1976 demonstrates the desirability for long advance planning. It is not too soon to turn our minds to the 200th anniversary of the document signed in Philadelphia almost exactly 191 years ago. We take considerable pride, and I think appropriately, in the fact that we have functioned as a nation under this one written constitution for nearly two centuries. No other nation can match that.

The events of the past 40 years have brought home to us very forcefully that freedom is fragile. This is particularly true of the freedom of our open society where we not only permit, but at times almost seem to invite attacks, because of our commitment to flexibility and change and our dedication to the values protected by the First Amendment. Eric Hoffer, with his uncomplicated logic and simplicity of style, has expressed his deep concern that our system of government and our free society may be more fragile in many respects than other societies, and he has suggested that "the social body" is perhaps more vulnerable and fragile than the human body.

It has been an article of faith with us that the artificial and manipulated systems of authoritarian regimes, no matter how strong they seem for a time, do not possess the powers of restoration or recuperation possessed by our kind of government. It is within the memory of all of us that a great many people in the 1930s, and even later, accepted Hitler's boast that he was creating a "1,000 year Reich." They remembered, too, that even before Hitler, as well as in more recent times, other people saw Soviet communism as "the wave of the future." It was Lincoln Steffens who said after a visit to Russia that he had "been over into the future and it works."

Surely the events of the last 40 or more years in world history underscore the importance of both the philosophy of freedom and the mechanisms and practices we have set up to insure a continuance of freedom.

We are surely committed to a significant celebration of

the creation of our constitutional system under the Constitution, which in 200 years took us from three million struggling pioneers into a great world power, and individual initiative was the secret of this success. It is, therefore, not too early to begin thinking and planning to be sure that what we do will be an appropriate recognition of the importance of the event and to serve as a guide to correct whatever flaws we see and to plan for the years ahead.

I submit that an appropriate way to do this will be to reexamine each of the three major articles of our organic law and compare the functions as they have been performed in recent times with the functions contemplated in 1787 by the men at Philadelphia. The Constitution was, of course, intended to be a mechanism to allow for the evolution of governmental institutions and constitutional concepts. But we should examine the changes which have occurred over two centuries and ask ourselves whether they are faithful to the spirit and the letter of the Constitution, or whether, with some, we have gone off on the wrong track.

This undertaking is too serious, too broad in scope and too important to be accomplished within one year. I suggest for your consideration, and to those with similar interests, that we set aside, not one year or even two years, but three years for this enterprise. Although the sequence need not be rigid, I would suggest that in 1985 we devote ourselves to an examination of Article I; in 1986, we should address the powers delegated by Article II; in 1987, we should address Article III. Let me briefly suggest a few of the differences between the expectations of the framers and present-day practices, bearing in mind Marshall's statement that the Constitution was "Intended to endure for ages to come, and consequently, to be adapted to the various crises in human affairs."

Under Article I, all legislative powers were vested in the Congress of the United States, or as Jefferson said, "the great council of the nation." It does not require the skills of historians or political scientists to observe that Congress in 1978 is a very different institution from what was contemplated in 1787. But we must do more than study how the Congress of today is different; we should proceed to assess whether the Congress is functioning according to the spirit of the founding fathers, even as we recognize that changes were inevitable with changing times and new problems.

What are the kind of changes that ought to be looked at? Surely, the growth factor is one. The House of Representatives has grown from 45 to 435; the Senate from 26 to 100. In the original contemplation, membership in the Congress was not to be a full-time occupation. The framers anticipated part-time public service of the leading citizens of each state. They were to come to Philadelphia (and later to Washington) for only a few months out of the year and spend the remaining seven or eight months back home on a farm or at a law practice or lumber mill. Now, it is a full-time profession—and necessarily so—given what we ask of them.

Obviously members of the Congress cannot be expected to function today as they did in the time of Clay, Calhoun and Webster when there were no typewriters, no computers, and when both communication and travel were very different from the present day. But some of the changes which we now observe in the functioning of the Congress are so fundamental that they can profitably be reexamined in light of original expectations about the functioning of the Legislative branch. For at least the first 100 years, each member of Congress could do all his own homework very largely as members of the British House of Commons still do. Each diligent member of Congress could readily read every bill proposed and understand what was being presented. Members of Congress are now torn between their mounting obligations to assist individual constituents in their dealings with the bureaucracy—to respond to mail—and the demands of the numerous subcommittees and committees upon which they serve. The mail is increased—perhaps—by new word processing equipment available to interest groups, with one set of word processing machines communicating with another machine. Added to all this is the constant need to mend political fences—which, of course, is democracy at work. .

These cross-pressures, the immense increase in the volume of legislative business and the need to match the size and specialized capabilities of the Executive branch experts accounts in large measure for the enormous expansion of congressional staffs. Indeed, some say that Congress is now not 535 persons but rather 535 plus thousands of staff members in the House and Senate. The *Congressional Quarterly weekly report* tells us that currently the congressional staffs aggregate about 16,500. The increase in the size of staffs seems to have induced some proliferation of the number of lobbyists—or perhaps it was the other way around. The number of corporations maintaining offices in Washington has grown in 15 years from about 50 to 300. More than 16,000 trade associations and labor unions have offices in this capital.

But the central focus in reexamination of the operations under Article I are the new problems which have added to the burdens of the Congress. Observers say that floor debate no longer occupies the role it did in times past. Members of Congress tend to become specialists—concentrating on the work of their own committees—rather than the generalists of an earlier day. A large part of the work of congressional staffs is devoted to "servicing" constituents entirely apart from the legislative process itself. This may be an appropriate part of the democratic ethos, but it is surely some distance from what the authors of the Constitution intended. This is not said critically but rather as the reality of present day life. Indeed my reflections on this subject rest on what members of Congress have said—publicly and privately.

A well-informed and highly sophisticated journalist, Elizabeth Drew, recently described the dilemma of members

of Congress attempting to cope with the flood of bills submitted and the lesser but still overwhelming flood of proposals emerging from committees. Many members of Congress have stated that it is almost impossible for any member
to read all the proposed legislation. Some critics suggest
that the increase in staffs has led directly to this increase in
the number and length of proposed bills and committee
reports. I do not know. But it is possible that a senator with
a staff of 50 or 60 or 70 persons may have more burdens
than benefits given the inexorable workings of Parkinson's
law. I do observe that rather than having their workload
lessened, Congressmen seem to find themselves overwhelmed
and many are retiring prematurely. We also see what perhaps is another result of current operations, and that is a
legislative product where, all too often, the meaning and
intent of Congress are blurred and the entire policy issue
winds up in the courts for resolution. And often the courts
have great difficulty discerning the true intent of Congress.

The purpose of these observations is neither to challenge
nor to criticize the process. It is simply to point out the
world of difference between functions contemplated in 1787
and the reality of 1978. A full year is needed to make a
concentrated analysis by political scientists, historians, and
other specialists—and members of Congress—to stimulate a
serious national discussion. Such an analysis can be made in
a more orderly and rational way if the discussion of one
branch is conducted entirely independent of discussion of
the other two branches. It is, therefore, desirable to set
aside the year 1985 for comprehensive reexamination of the
Article I functions.

The operations of the Executive branch, like those of
the Congress, have also undergone dramatic evolution and
change. In 1789 there was only a handful of "executives" in
the Executive branch along with customs collectors and
postmasters. The total budget of the Federal Government
in dollars was smaller by far at the beginning than that of
a modest sized city—Colorado Springs—for example. Com-

munication between the first Executive and the Legislative branch was casual and informal.

Although the members of the first Supreme Court wisely resisted President Washington's request for advisory opinions and declined to perform other functions which they deemed to be executive in nature, there is little doubt that Chief Justice Jay gave advice to Washington over the dinner table and even in writing. The President had no professional staff for himself. His close advisors also included the cabinet secretaries and the Vice President.

Although the Executive branch grew greatly from 1789 to the first World War, our wartime President, Woodrow Wilson, pecked away at his Hammond typewriter, turning out speeches and messages to Congress—and an outline of the League of Nations.

President Hoover had three or four staff aides, then called "secretaries," who assisted him with his problems, including one former Congressman who presumably handled legislative relations. Franklin Roosevelt, as a candidate, attacked Hoover for his excessively large staff. Yet, as we know, the great expansion of the White House staff began under President Franklin Roosevelt as the whole Executive branch burgeoned to meet the emergencies created by the worldwide depression. Thus one matter to be reflected upon in 1986 is the implications of the size of the Executive branch. Another question deserving analysis is what we now understand from the provision of Article II stating that the Executive power shall be vested in the President. Today Executive power is actually in the hands of a few thousand of nearly three million civilian employees of the Executive branch. There are 150,000 employees in the Department of Health, Education and Welfare alone—more than the standing army of the country in early parts of this century.

There are other changes. For nearly a half century the Executive branch initiated much of the significant legislation. It is interesting to note that the Civil Service Commission is holding a workshop this december—and I use the Commission's language—to "help train agency personnel who will be assuming assignments in the formulation of legislation." This is entirely appropriate but it perhaps in part explains why Congress needed specialist staffs to cope with the Executive. The growth in the rule-making activity of the federal agencies has given rise to concern and indeed to challenges by recent Presidents who thought their policies were being frustrated.

One example of changes brought on in the electronic age is the relationship of President with the media. Perhaps we should ask whether any President should be expected to have at his fingertips, and on the top of his head, a comprehensive and totally accurate response to every question submitted from an audience consisting of several hundred politically sophisticated media reporters? At times we read a superficial comparison to the British system where the prime Minister and his cabinet ministers appear in the Commons for the question period. But the comparison is flawed because in Britain there is a fixed agenda for the question period. The Prime Minister or any member of his cabinet need be well-informed only on the specific and limited subjects covered by that agreed agenda.

Is it possible that the media, the Presidency, and the nation would be better served if presidential press conferences were—at least—confined to agreed subjects—for example, the problems of the Middle East, or inflation or energy—rather than having every press conference open to the entire range of problems confronting the country. The evening news and the morning papers would be able to focus with greater clarity and in greater depth on particular policy issues and the media might thus be better able to inform the public in the long run.

These are just a sample of some of the issues and problems which might be discussed during the year 1986 by political scientists, historians, journalists, and those who have actual first-hand experience in government. Others having broader experience in government will see many areas for inquiry.

Questions about the present functioning of the Judiciary compared with original expectations could be dealt with in 1987. Since I cannot qualify either as a totally expert witness on the subject or as totally unbiased, I will leave it to others to flesh out the full scope of the inquiry for there is a long list of questions deserving serious study.

I suspect that by the time the delegates reached Article III that they were getting weary in the hot and humid Philadelphia summer. The entire Judicial article contains only 369 words. The first Judiciary Act of 1789 authorized 13 US District Judges and six members of the Supreme Court. Perhaps the feeling of those weary delegates at the Constitutional Convention was that a branch of government which would consist initially of only 19 judges did not call for much rhetoric—or much attention. The Constitution provided that the federal courts would have a limited and special function—in that day largely deciding admiralty cases.

The number of judges has grown from those first 19 to 397 authorized District Judges, 97 judges of the Courts of Appeals, and another 21 judges of three specialized tribunals—a total of 515. Another 130 senior judges continue to serve—fortunately for us. This number will soon increase by approximately 150 when Congress passes the Omnibus Judgeship Bill—which may happen this week [September 1978].

The Supreme Court has increased from six justices to nine, remaining at that figure for over a century. I do not know of anyone advocating increasing the membership of the Supreme Court—least of all the present justices. One wag commented that nine members of the Supreme Court have produced sufficient mischief in this country and any increase would be intolerable.

With 19 federal judges in 1789—and for at least 100 years—there were no significant "management" problems.

Even with the 100 or more judges during the time Taft was Chief Justice, the management problem was not enormous. But Taft saw into the future and fought for the creation of the Conference of Senior Circuit Judges now (the Judicial Conference of the United States) to assist in "managing" the business of the courts," as he called it. The administrative office of the United States courts was created in 1939 with essentially housekeeping functions. The Federal Judicial Center began operations in 1968 as the research, development and educational arm of the Judiciary. In 1971 the position of Circuit Executive—a management assistant for the chief circuit judges—was created for each circuit. We must also count supporting personnel—court clerks, bailiffs, court reporters and so forth, or a total of 9,377 persons. We see, therefore, that the Judicial branch, while small, has increased greatly since 1789.

For nearly nine years congress has failed to create a single new judgeship and the courts have had to cope with the enormous increase in workload with additional law clerks and staff lawyers. The pressure of caseloads has led to an increase in the proportion of cases decided without oral argument and often without a formal, written opinion. Lawyers oppose this.

Some responsible and well-informed lawyers and scholars have criticized the increasing complexity of judicial procedure arguing that overuse of pre-trial processes complicate and delay trials. Others have echoed the criticism, made first by Roscoe Pound in 1906, that the excesses of the adversary system hinder rather than promote the ends of justice. The processes of administrative law are being challenged and questions are raised as to the soundness of trying complex anti-trust cases before 12 lay jurors picked at random from the population.

These developments inspire a series of questions, questions about the efficiency of courts functioning under such demands, questions about the growth of a judicial "bureaucracy," and even questions about the duties placed on the

Chief Justice are emerging. Should it be expected that the Chief Justice, with all the duties of other justices of the court, be called upon to be the "Chief Executive" of the Judicial branch. Congress made the Chief Justice Chairman of the Judicial Conference of the United States with duties that absorb hundreds of hours each year. It made him Chairman of the Federal Judicial Center, with similar time demands. These two organizations are expected to develop innovative programs and mechanisms to improve and speed up justice. Because Chief Justices have somehow been able to manage up to now does not mean this can continue to be true in the third century under the Constitution. Seven years ago a committee of distinguished lawyers and scholars, chaired by Professor Paul Freund of Harvard, recommended that another court be created to take part of the work now resting on the Supreme Court. No action has been taken on that proposal.

There are serious questions as to how long justices can work a sixty-hour week and maintain appropriate standards.

At least as important as the need to examine the increase in the size of the Judicial branch is the need to examine the powers exercised by the Judiciary. The authors of the Constitution did not contemplate that the Judiciary would be an overseer of the other two branches. At most, they expected that the judicial function would be confined to interpreting laws and deciding whether particular acts of the Congress or of the Executive were in conflict with the Constitution, but even that was not explicit. Surely, that is all Marshall's opinion in *Marbury* v *Madison* means.

Paradoxically, in recent years, the Supreme Court has been subjected to criticism from both ends of the spectrum. On the one hand, there are critics who suggest that the Supreme Court, like the other two branches, has become "imperial" in the sense of exercising powers not assigned to it by the Constitution. On the other hand, there are those who say that the Supreme Court has been too passive and has not undertaken to engage in wide ranging social and political activism thought by some to be called for by contemporary problems. It will be for others to evaluate these contentions. All this is rich fodder for symposia in 1987.

We make a large point of the independence and separateness of the three branches, but the authors of the Constitution also contemplated that there would be coordination between the branches deriving from a common purpose. That they should consult on some matters is beyond doubt. How far that should go is a subject for careful study.

The uniqueness and true genius of the document is that it has precluded any one of the branches from dominating any other. This will continue so long as we are faithful to the spirit and letter of the Constitution.

Project '87 is already underway and the Judicial Conference of the United States last year authorized the appointment of a special committee to prepare for an observance of this significant historic event. If we—collectively—use the "lead time" now available to us, we can develop a program worthy of the importance of the occasion.

Although none of us can alone determine the totality of what the Bicentennial of 1787 should be, you—here today—are uniquely qualified to evaluate the merits of this proposal and to help with its implementation if you find merit in it.

If we concentrate along these lines for one year on each of the three branches and their functions, perhaps with the latter part of the third year devoted to an overview of all that has been discussed, debated and analyzed in the preceding years, conceivably we may produce a series of papers comparable in utility, if not in quality, with the Federalist Papers of 200 years ago.

Whatever the program is to be, the time to begin planning is now.

NOTES ON THE SITUATION: A CRITIQUE[1]

GRIFFIN B. BELL[2]

On January 25, 1979, Griffin Bell, then Attorney General delivered the J. A. Vickers Sr. Memorial Lecture in the University Theatre at the University of Kansas in Lawrence. The lecture was one in a series that had been established to enable the university to bring to the campus prominent citizens "to debate or discuss subjects vital to maintaining a free political and market society."

When the Attorney General of the United States, in a Democratic administration, speaks forth to advocate less government regulation, it should make news. Historically, the Democratic party has pushed for more governmental intervention in American life and the Republican party, in the main, has resisted the push. In his speech at the University of Kansas, Griffin Bell declared the "evergrowing bureaucracy to be more than a painful nuisance, it is a prescription for societal suicide," a statement that sounds as if it had been stolen from Arizona Republican Barry Goldwater.

The strategy of the speech deserves attention. Bell insisted that he was speaking as "a concerned citizen schooled in public service, and *not* as a spokesman for the Administration." But in light of the fact that he is a trusted adviser and long-time political friend of President Carter, what Bell said must be regarded as consistent with the administration's position. In fact, he was probably attempting to meet the challenge presented by the swelling movement for restricting government spending, including a proposed constitutional amendment requiring a balanced budget.

The speech possesses a well constructed need-plan structure, with a majority of it devoted to a six-point solution for reducing or curbing the bureaucracy. But into each suggestion, he cleverly inserts much factual information concerning the area of government he is discussing. One question worth considering is whether the introduction was appropriate. Can the military occupation of the South during Reconstruction be fairly compared to the per-

[1] Delivered as the J. A. Vickers Sr., Memorial Lecture, the University Theatre, University of Kansas, Lawrence, Kansas, at 6 P.M., January 25, 1979.
[2] For biographical note, see Appendix.

vasiveness of the present federal bureaucracy? Perhaps the speaker
was striving more for dramatic effect than for appropriateness
and, of course, the use of the reference in opening and closing the
speech unified it.

Benjamin Harvey Hill was a distinguished Georgian
who did his best prior to the Civil War to prevent the
secession of Georgia from the Union. Having lost, he joined
in the Confederacy. Following the War and Reconstruction, he became a United States Senator from Georgia, but
it was during the Reconstruction that he became prominent
by reason of a series of newspaper columns entitled, *Notes
on the Situation*. I have appropriated that title for my remarks tonight.

What happened to the South during the Reconstruction
is a subject of continuing interest to political scientists as
well as to historians. It was a period when one part of our
country was under occupation by the armed forces of the
nation. It was a period during which the national Congress
engaged in a concerted effort to reconstitute the political
and economic structure of the conquered territory.

We have no occupation as such today, but the entire
nation—not just the South—is presently regulated by a
force more pervasive and more powerful than all the Union
armies of the Reconstruction. That force is the federal
bureaucracy, which by laws and regulations, by orders and
printed forms, and by a thousand other unseen methods
subjects all of us to some degree of federal scrutiny and
control.

It will be my thesis tonight that if the Republic is to
remain viable, we must find ways to curb, and then to reduce, this government by bureaucracy. We must return to
government by directly accountable public officials—local,
state, and federal. The only other alternative, I predict, is
to have an increasingly costly and inefficient form of government, wholly removed from democratic control—and I use
the lower case "d" in democratic here! When our society
is threatened from within and without by such awesome

problems as inflation, military aggression, poverty, and world famine, this evergrowing bureaucracy is more than a painful nuisance: it is a prescription for societal suicide.

In elaborating on this thesis, I speak to you from the vantage point of a public official, one who has served in the federal Judiciary and who now serves in the Executive branch. My observations are not those of a political scientist or an historian, although I claim to be an amateur in each field.

Obviously, for the next half hour, I will be speaking to you as a concerned citizen schooled in public service and *not* as a spokesman for the administration. These thoughts are definitely my own—as you will shortly hear!

Let me begin by noting my credentials to criticize the federal bureaucracy. As Attorney General I am in charge of some 55,000 employees within the Justice Department, who are spread over 23 separate component offices, bureaus, and divisions. Our budget, which is small by comparison, will come to about two and one-half billion dollars for fiscal year 1979.

I am not alone in concluding that the unchecked growth of the federal bureaucracy may be a mortal threat to our historic forms of government. New York's Senator Daniel Patrick Moynihan, the eminent scholar and former ambassador to India, gave a memorable address last March in New York City, in which he spoke of the imperial presidency, the imperial Congress, and even the imperial judiciary. He concluded that the inevitable concomitant of "imperial" government was the spread of bureaucracy from the executive branch to the legislative and the judicial branches as well. If I may quote from that speech: ". . . the long run effect will be to create government by submerged horizontal bureaucracies that link the three branches of government, speaking their own private language, staying in place while their Constitutional masters come and go."

It is in the vein of Senator Moynihan's remarks that I speak to you tonight about our federal government. The restlessness of the American people is now manifesting itself in the notion of calling a Constitutional Convention through an application from two-thirds of the state legislatures. The Founding Fathers gave us this alternative way of amending the Constitution, doubtless foreseeing that the people might some day lose control of the federal government and even of the Congress to the extent that they could not achieve their will.

This state of governmental affairs is worth pondering. Lack of control has a good deal to do with the scourge of inflation, fueled in part by government spending; it has much to do with the present flood of stultifying federal regulations; and it has much to do with citizen frustration, caused by a seeming inability to govern ourselves.

A recent *Wall Street Journal* editorial made the clearest statement about this phenomenon:

There is a clear sense in this country that government has become highly wasteful of resources and too big and internally contentious to respond to changing circumstances and needs. The time required to get the necessary government clearances and build a single electric power plant in the U.S. is now triple the length of the time the U.S. needed to mobilize for and fight World War II.

That is a cold and sober observation.

Senator Moynihan has provided us with a short and accurate description of the problem, but few have gone beyond rhetorical attacks on that problem. It has been often said that it is better to light one candle than to curse the darkness. As a lawyer, I put it in different terms in stating that one should not rail at the law. By the same token, we should not rail at the government; rather our approach should be to correct the government.

Therefore, I would like to make a few modest suggestions which, hopefully, may assist in turning the tide.

These suggestions are in the nature of refurbishment. They in no way undermine or even disparage our system. They are corrective in nature and are asserted under our duty as citizens to seek to improve the system. It is through such duty that we replenish our democracy under our constitutional system.

As a first step, I would amend the Constitution to provide one six-year term for the President. This is certainly not a new idea, having been originally proposed in Congress in 1826 and reintroduced some 160 times since then. It has been advocated by several Presidents. But it is an idea whose time may have come. This change will enable a President to devote 100 percent of his or her attention to the office. No time would be spent in seeking reelection. Under the present system, the President serves three years and then must spend a substantial part of the fourth year in running for reelection, assuming a President decides to seek reelection.

Moreover, the current four year term is actually too short to achieve any of the major changes and improvements that a President should accomplish. The funding cycles are so long that it is well into a President's third year before his own program changes take effect. This leaves the bureaucracy in control.

A single six-year term would permit the long-term, steady planning and implementation that our government needs, plus saving that fourth year now lost to campaigning.

Second, I would propose a complete review and reduction of the regulating and litigating authority of the independent federal agencies. The President has the authority now to curb those departments within the Executive branch of the government, but, to the surprise of most Americans, the independent agencies such as the Federal Trade Commission, the Consumer Products Safety Commission, and the Nuclear Regulatory Commission are all wholly separate and not subject to his control at all. Most have the power to promulgate regulations and rules that affect all of us, and many have the statutory power to litigate in the name of the United States, even when the positions being advocated by them are contrary to those taken by the Department of Justice. And their regulations are legion and growing every day.

Third, I would place a severe restriction on the staffs allocated to the President, the Congress, and even the federal courts. More staff invariably means more time in which to evolve more ideas about how to increase government control over the lives of the American people. But at the same time we make this move, we as citizens must also lower our own expectations about government. In large measure, the size of government has grown because we have all benefited at one time or another from some federal programs. The temptation is overwhelming to ask that the federal government pay for this project or to support that program, because then the average citizen cannot so easily perceive the linkage between the service delivered and the price paid in terms of the incremental federal tax dollars. Local officials and local citizens alike praise the award of federal grants to local communities, but they fail to recognize that such aid builds the federal bureaucracy and furthers the loss of local government control and responsibility.

As a former federal judge and now as Attorney General, in charge of our 3,800 lawyers in the Justice Department, I can personally testify to the growth of the federal judiciary and its increased own role in our lives. Again, this growth stems mostly from the desires of the American people, who now turn to the courts—and especially the federal courts—at the slightest provocation. The caseload in turn fuels the demands for more and more judges and more and more support staff. The citizenry must reaffirm its commitment to other and more informal dispute resolution devices, or it cannot rightly complain when the judiciary, like its sister branches, continues to increase in size in response to cries for more services.

Fourth, I would urge Congress to sharply curtail, if not abolish, the so-called "rule-making" powers of the independent regulatory commissions. To most of you in this audience tonight, the concept of "rule-making" might sound as though it were simply a procedural device, used to set out the rules under which a particular agency might conduct itself. That is far from the way that term is used in Washington! In truth, rule-making is a total substitute for all other forms of government, executive, legislative, and even judicial. Its abuse can stymie and frustrate the government of whole states and the operations of entire industries.

A classic case was presented to me while I was a Circuit Judge on the 5th Circuit. The State of Texas had, pursuant to federal law, produced a state plan to control smog within the limits set down by federal regulations. The Environmental Protection Agency—or EPA, as we call it—disapproved the Texas plan and issued under its rule-making powers its own plan, which incorporated the Texas controls and a host of other more stringent requirements. To our surprise, we found that the EPA had established its standards for Texas largely on a study done for the Los Angeles, California, region, and that that study had been performed 15 years earlier, so as to be totally out of date. Yet, but for our order to the EPA, the citizens of Texas would today still be paying for a set of air quality controls promulgated by a set of faceless bureaucrats in Washington, based on a contracted study from Los Angeles, 15 years out of date. *That* is rule-making.

Of course, once the rule is made by an agency, all interested parties are given the right to comment. But the point is that rule-making has none of the safeguards of the legislative process and yet also is a non-adversary proceeding.

Fifth, I would urge strong support for President Carter's plans to reduce the volume, complexity, and cost of government regulations generally. As Attorney General, charged with enforcing the nation's laws, I have seen so much burden cast upon our citizens by the host of regulations. Federal regulations currently in force cover about 60,000 printed pages with thousands more in interpretations and guidelines. They are often written in defiance of the English language. Many of these regulations have retarded our real economic growth, by impairing our efforts to improve the productivity of labor and capital. And the paperwork and compliance burden on the smaller American businesses is simply impossible, so that the net result is wholesale disobedience, which then breeds disrespect for the law generally. If large numbers of our people begin to ignore our law, we will lose that cohesive attitude which has so symbolized our country and which has saved our Republic from anarchy and ruin on countless occasions.

For these reasons, the President has ordered the reduction in the number of regulations and a simplification of their reporting requirements. Thus far, the number of reporting hours has been reduced by 85 million hours per year, or about 10 percent—which is equivalent to the work of 50,000 people for one year. He has also required major new regulations to be accompanied by a comprehensive cost-benefit study, so that the social and economic merits can be weighed against the likely costs. That, too, will reduce the number and complexity of regulations. Necessary and proper regulations will be continued but at the least expensive and burdensome level. And this will help in the fight against inflation, because each incremental cost added to a product or service by a new and perhaps unnecessary regulation further erodes the buying power of the American dollar. Such a watch over the cost of new regulations might be termed an "inflation impact statement."

And, *sixth,* we need to restore confidence and non-partisan support to some of the fundamental units of the federal government. It is interesting to note that three Cabinet officials were exempted by the President from attending the recent mini-convention of the Democratic Party in Memphis: the Secretary of Defense, the Secretary of State, and the Attorney General. That suggests to me that these officers and their departments have to be seen as non-partisan, charged to work under neutral principles of law and policy. There is no room in our federal system for the vagaries and viscissitudes of partisan politics in the conduct of our national defense or our foreign relations; in like fashion, the laws of our land must be enforced without fear or favor as to party affiliation.

I mention this last fact, not because it relates to my earlier observations about bureaucracy, but because these three arms of the executive branch are the guardians of our freedoms. It is through their independence and professionalism that we American citizens have the liberties—and even license—to debate and discuss how our government is to be run. So in their strength lies the strength of the American people.

I can tell you that we at the Justice Department have tried very hard over the last two years to erase the ugly stains of the Watergate era and to create a truly independent, professional organization. I am proud that from the FBI to the DEA to our litigating divisions, we have accomplished that goal. We operate by and fully in accordance with the law, on a non-partisan basis, as President Carter pledged to do when he took office. That will be the pledge of the Department from now on.

As I said at the beginning of these remarks, I am speaking as an American citizen proud of his country's achievements over two centuries and yet fearful of what lies ahead for his nation. We have come to a crossroad in the history of this land—politically, morally, and philosophically. Each of us must now decide who, if anyone, shall be given this enormous power over our lives.

I have often said that the wisest use of power is not to use it at all. But if such power must be used, use it sparingly. That is the prescription I would write for our federal government today, for the temptation of great power may otherwise be too great to resist. As Abraham Lincoln so aptly put it in 1837, "I believe it is universally understood and acknowledged that all men will ever act correctly, unless they have a motive to do otherwise."

President Carter and I share a common conviction that it is time to return government to the people. We believe that we have no roving commissions to do good, that such an attitude on the part of government constitutes a gross abuse of power. Our administration is committed to devolving power back to the people of this country, to save the nation from its own ever-growing government.

So, in closing, let me once again refer to Benjamin Harvey Hill, that distinguished Georgian and American, whose statue in the Georgia State House bears this inscription: "Who saves his country saves himself, saves all things and all things saved do bless him. Who lets his country die lets all things die, dies himself ignobly and all things dying curse him." Thank you.

THE BUDGET AND INFLATION

PROPOSALS FOR CHANGE: AN INAUGURAL ADDRESS [1]

EDMUND G. BROWN JR.[2]

The tax revolt has been gathering steam since the California voters passed the now-famous Proposition 13 which limited property taxes. First Governor Jerry Brown was an opponent of tax reform; now he has become a leading advocate of cutting taxes and balancing the federal budget. In his re-election inaugural address, January 8, 1979, he startled the nation by proposing a billion dollar reduction of the California budget, a reduction of 5,000 state employees, and a constitutional amendment to balance the federal budget or a constitutional convention to achieve this goal. Although the address was a broad comment on the times, its greatest significance was that it made Brown the leading proponent of tax reform and perhaps a serious contender for the 1980 Democratic presidential nomination.

In evaluating Brown's daring move, Paul Priole, Republican leader in the California Assembly, put the situation in perspective: "The Governor's got an issue that has made him a national figure. I think the Governor, having assumed the leadership on this issue, will not have any credibility if he cannot pass it in his own state. Obviously, if Jerry Brown is unable to succeed with his proposal, he's no longer a problem for President Carter."

James Reston of the New York *Times,* a keen observer of American politics, concludes that

> this rumpled, talkative, serious young man now approaching his 41st birthday, is not only challenging Jimmy Carter for the Presidency, but also calling for a political, technological, and moral reappraisal of American life. . . . He is still the most interesting if the most unpredictable personality in American politics today, and . . . he will . . . bring some new and arresting questions into the Presidential campaign of 1980.

[1] Delivered at inaugural ceremonies at the Capitol, Sacramento, California, January 8, 1979. Quoted by permission. Title supplied by editor.
[2] For biographical note, see Appendix.

The new year on which we now begin [1979] is a year of testing. Once again our economy is careening down the path of inflation that inexorably leads to recession. At such a time, it is right to reexamine our assumptions, state clearly our goals, and work confidently for the future.

1979 is the international year of the child. Those born this year will graduate in the class of 2000. What they inherit will depend on the courage and vision we pass on to them. Whether Californians in that year are up among the best or stagnating in the continuing aftershocks of obsolete technology and pervasive foreign imports, that depends on us.

Today we see the ethos of our moment dominated by "getting and spending" rather than innovation and risk. The depressing spirit of the age ungratefully feeds off the boldness of the past. Where there should be saving for the future, I see frantic borrowing. Where there should be investment in productive capacity, I see frenetic consumption.

California has been called the great exception. From the mystic aura of the name itself to the conquest of outer space, California has inspired greatness among its many immigrant people. Gold, forests, rich agricultural fields, high technology, universities of excellence, the Pacific horizon, diverse ethnic groups—all these have converged to keep our state a dream for the hundreds of thousands who still cross our borders each year. In the last four years, 1.5 million jobs have been created and the proportion of people over 16 employed in the wage economy has grown from 56 percent to 61 percent, a participation rate matched rarely anywhere in this country or anywhere else in the world. Over 14 million motor vehicles each month set new records in gallons of gasoline consumed and miles driven over our roads. Our 22 million people produce each year more than the combined effort of the billion people who inhabit India, Pakistan, Indonesia, the Philippines, South Korea, Nigeria, and Zaire. We have the most advanced technology, the most stringent environmental laws, a strong legal commitment to equality, the highest transfer payments to those who depend on government, and the most advanced labor laws.

Yet the mistrust of our public institutions and mere anxiety about our future economy are more the order than the exception. Three quarters of the people do not trust their government. More than half of the eligible citizens of California again decided not to vote in the last election. Why? Why the anti-government mood? I asked this same question four years ago and now I believe I understand. Simply put, the citizens are revolting against a decade of political leaders who righteously spoke against inflation and excessive government spending but who in practice pursued the opposite course.

It is in this fundamental contradiction between what political leaders have said in their anti-inflation and anti-spending speeches and what they have actually done in their fiscal policies that we find the cause of today's political malaise. The ordinary citizen knows that government contributes to inflation and that runaway inflation is as destructive to our social wellbeing as an invading army.

The economists will argue about the fine points but the people know that something is profoundly wrong when 75 percent of government spending decisions are automatically decided by past formulas and not present lawmakers—formulas that ensure that government and its taxes always keep ahead of inflation.

People know that something is wrong when the federal government stimulates inflation and inflation raises the face value of prices, income and property, so that the taxes on each grow higher and higher. This perverse government money machine has created a fiscal dividend for local, state, and federal government and allowed all three to expand faster than inflation and faster than real economic growth. These unauthorized dividends are now being cancelled. The tax revolt is being heard.

There is much to learn about the unprecedented primary vote and victory of Proposition 13. Not the least of which is that the established political union, and corporate powers are no match for an angry citizenry recoiling against an inflationary threat to their homes and pocketbooks.

While it is true that the tax revolt has increased the privileges of the few, it has without question inspired the hopes of many. Plain working people, the poor, the elderly, those on fixed incomes, those who cannot keep up with each new round of inflation or protect themselves from each subsequent round of recession, these are the people who are crying out for relief.

But in their name and in the name of misfortune of every kind, false prophets have risen to advocate more and more government spending as the cure—more bureaucratic programs and higher staffing ratios of professional experts. They have told us that billion dollar government increases are really deep cuts from the yet higher levels of spending they demand and that attempts to limit the inflationary growth of government derive not from wisdom but from selfishness. That disciplining government reflects not a care for the future but rather self-absorption. These false prophets, I tell you, can no longer distinguish the white horse of victory from the pale horse of death.

In this decade, government at all levels has increased spending faster than the true rate of economic growth, taxes per $100 of income have climbed steadily. The cure for inflation has been administered with a vengeance. Yet most people feel worse, not better, about their government benefactor. The elderly find their fixed incomes eroding in half; those about to retire fear their future pensions will never keep pace. Ten million California workers see their wages rise but not as fast as prices. Those on welfare obtain larger grants but find more expensive groceries.

It is time to get off the treadmill, to challenge the assumption that more government spending automatically leads to better living. The facts prove otherwise. More and more inflationary spending leads to decline abroad and decadence at home. Ultimately it will unwind the social compact that forms the basis of our society.

Lord Keynes, in whose name many of the false prophets claim to speak, had this to say on the subject:

By a process of inflation, governments can confiscate, secretly and unobserved, an important part of the wealth of their citizens. By this method they not only confiscate, but they confiscate arbitrarily; and, while the process impoverishes many, it actually enriches some. . . . There is no subtler, no surer means of overturning the existing basis of society than to debauch the currency. The process engages all the hidden forces of economic law on the side of destruction, and does it in a manner which not one man in a million is able to diagnose.

Government, no less than the individual, must live within limits. It is time to bring our accounts into balance. Government, as exemplar and teacher, must manifest a self-discipline that spreads across the other institutions in our society, so that we can begin to work for the future, not just consume the present.

I propose that this year the state government lower the amount of taxes it collects per $100 of income to the level of four years ago. This will require a billion dollar tax cut. Such a tax reduction should, on a percentage basis, give the greatest benefit to renters and those at the lower and middle level of the income scale. A flat tax credit combined with an increase in renter assistance will accomplish this goal.

Some might ask, how did the state obtain this billion dollars? Did the state extract it from new wealth or increased production? Was there a vote of the legislature to levy a new tax? No! Quite simply the perverse money machine of inflation is artificially raising income, property, prices, and profits and combining with pre-existing state law to generate a tax windfall. Unearned, unvoted, and undeserved.

Next, I propose that for the first time since World War II, we actually decrease the number of positions in state government. A reduction of 5,000 is reasonable and attainable without significant layoffs. It will mean that in

1980 we will operate government with fewer employees than we did in 1977.

I see this as state government, not working less, but becoming more productive. Jobs in government, education, and health constitute a substantial part of the work done in our state. Yet, it is in these fields where productivity is declining. Each year government employment grows. Each year we spend more money on fewer students. Each year we increase dramatically the amount spent on medical care. Are we better governed? Are we better educated? Are we healthier? Perhaps, but not commensurate with the additional dollars and taxes spent on each. The time has come for California to pioneer and increase productivity in these fields. It is a myth that services such as government, teaching, and curing lay fundamentally beyond those processes which have created our modern agriculture, our electronics, and aerospace. Our higher standard of living comes directly from work that uses the latest tools and the most imagination. Unless we improve the way we learn, the way we heal, and the way we govern, it is inevitable that our standard and quality of life will decline.

We are in the midst of an information revolution that draws its center from the computer and communication industries of California. As the power of the human mind expands through the technology of our own state, the challenge will be to use the new tools to expand learning, to prevent disease and make government leaner as it becomes more effective.

As government makes itself more productive, it must also strip away the roadblocks and the regulatory underbrush that it often mindlessly puts in the path of private citizens. Unneeded licenses and proliferating rules can stifle initiative, especially for small business. Society is more interdependent and our capacity to harm both nature and ourselves is greater than ever. Yet many regulations primarily protect the past, prop up privilege or prevent sensible economic choices.

These are the rules that should be changed in the on-going self-examination by each department of government. Where economic incentives, instead of rules, can accomplish the goal, they should be tried.

Finally, in order to ensure that we permanently slow the inflationary growth of government, I will support an appropriate constitutional amendment to limit state and local spending. Such measures are difficult to draft but are justified today in order to recapture a sense of the common interest as opposed to the narrow and special interests that combine to push spending beyond what is reasonable.

I will also support the resolution now pending before the legislature calling upon Congress to propose a constitutional amendment to balance the federal budget or to convene a constitutional convention to achieve this goal.

The roller coaster of inflation followed by recession is out of control. In the last 12 years, leaders of both parties have tried in vain to slow its reckless course. At the same time, states compete with each other to extract more and more federal grants that are financed out of the deficits and not the productivity of the nation. It is, therefore, right that these same states join together to demand a constitutional amendment that will serve as the occasion for finally restraining the inflationary spending of the federal government. The nation, no less than the individual states, must eventually balance its books. The excuse that only annual deficits promote full employment is refuted by the continuing decline in productivity and investment which form the only true base of long term employment.

A constitutional convention to propose an amendment to balance the budget is unprecedented, but so is the paralysis that prevents necessary action.

The time has finally come to balance what we spend with what we produce.

To truly achieve this, we must enlist the talent of all the people in our society. This is what I call investment in human capital—an investment we have yet to fully make.

Despite the affluence of California, too many still languish in the backwaters of our society.

We encounter each day the paradox of unfilled jobs existing side by side with unemployed or underemployed people. The challenge is to break down the remaining discriminatory barriers and encourage business, labor, and government to provide on-the-job training, apprenticeships, and full upward mobility. We can never reach our full capacity unless we liberate the human spirit and enfranchise all the people of our state—whatever their color, their language, their disability, their age or their sex. To more completely achieve this goal, I will support the necessary changes in our Fair Employment Practices Act, to include prohibitions against discrimination based on sexual preference. The diversity of our people can be a cause of hatred and anxiety or the source of strength and continued advancement. The choice is ours.

As we expand the opportunities for those within our borders, we must recognize the affinity that we have with those beyond. No small part of our present wealth or our future possibilities derives from our location on the Pacific rim. The trade and widening exchange with Mexico, with Canada, and with our more distant neighbors in the far east, offer potential still rarely imagined.

After the first Americans and long before most of our ancestors arrived in California, our neighbors from Mexico were naming our cities and dividing our lands. For too long we have ignored Mexico. Unless we understand that California and Mexico are linked by history, geography, families, and a common future, we will miss one of the great opportunities of the next decade.

Let us also not neglect the other forms of life and the natural systems on which we all depend. The soil, the sun, and the water make possible our forests and the wood we take from them, as well as the food that our farmers are able to produce. This timeless bounty will endure only if we have proper reverence and respect for our natural systems. The air can become cancerous, the water polluted, and the soil eroded. It is up to us to so manage growth and technology, that we enhance the quality of our environment, not undermine it to the loss of those who will come after us. Many a civilization has fallen with its forests and eroded with its soil.

I said that 1979 was a year of testing—testing whether these people that fill the freeways of California have the vision to prepare for the year 2000. Is Alexander Solzhenitsyn correct when he says that: "A decline in courage may be the most striking feature which an outside observer notices in the west in our days?" [Commencement Address, Harvard University, June 8, 1978.] Will we make the sacrifices to protect our land and to create the new energy sources that will power our factories? Will we invest in the information revolution and continue to dominate the conquest of outer space? Will we see beyond the stereotypes and embrace our human diversity?

To all of this I must answer with a resounding yes. California will build for the future, not steal from it. And as we do, we will know in our hearts patriotism is not just defending the country of our fathers, but preparing the land of our children.

"TOO MANY QUESTIONS . . . NOT ENOUGH ANSWERS" [1]

Edmund S. Muskie [2]

The bandwagon of the balance-the-budget constitutional amendment picked up considerable support since Governor Jerry Brown announced his support of it in his Inaugural Address, January 8, 1979 (published elsewhere in the volume). George Gallup and other public-opinion surveys estimate that eighty percent of the electorate favor the measure (*Christian Science Monitor*, February 6, 1979). One survey showed that thirty states may consider amending their constitutions to limit state and local taxes, twenty propose cutting property taxes, nineteen propose cutting income taxes, eleven are considering reducing sales taxes, and eleven favor reducing business taxes (*Wall Street Journal*, February 16, 1979). Predictions are that the necessary thirty-four states will pass petitions favoring the amendment of the federal constitution to mandate a balanced budget.

The tax revolt momentum has impressed many American leaders including Edward Kennedy, Democratic senator from Massachusetts, George Meany, AFL-CIO president, and Vernon E. Jordon, Jr., president of the Urban League. Jordon called the Brown proposals "nothing more than a modern version of the old snake oil remedies" (Brad Knickerbocker, *Christian Science Monitor*, February 6, 1979). With caution, the administration exercised quiet opposition to Brown's budget balancing proposals.

An excellent example of a rebuttal of Brown's argument is a speech that Edmund S. Muskie (Democrat, Maine) delivered before the National Press Club in Washington, D.C. on February 13, 1979. Well trained as a debater at Bates College and an effective speaker, Muskie poked holes in Brown's theory and raised important questions about the wisdom of a constitutional convention. In a sober tone, he pleaded for caution in considering the amendment of the Constitution to balance the budget. Basing his argument on historical precedent, he pointed out, one-by-one, the

---

[1] Delivered to the National Press Club at a luncheon, Washington, D.C., February 13, 1979. Quoted by permission. Title supplied by editor.

[2] For biographical note, see Appendix.

dangers implicit in tampering with the Constitution and ignoring plain fiscal discipline, as a solution to the problem.

In 1930—Franklin Delano Roosevelt confided to a friend —"It's becoming harder and harder for an honest fellow with a wife and children and nineteen servants to make a decent living."

In 1979, for families and governments alike, it is still often difficult to make ends meet. And the rush is on for a quick-fix approach to the government's fiscal dilemma.

Mathematicians have a saying—solutions can't be found until problems are stated correctly.

This afternoon, I don't expect to find the solution to the difficulties we face in balancing the budget. I do hope to state the problem correctly. I hope to raise some serious questions. I hope to start some serious people thinking— particularly about the growing demand for a new constitutional convention.

That movement has attracted much attention—but little careful thought. It is considered too casually by proponent and foe alike.

To be sure, some legislatures have reviewed this proposal with appropriate deliberation. But in many statehouses, prudence has given way to panic. Resolutions to change the Constitution of the United States are introduced at noon and adopted before dinner. Sometimes without a single hearing—without a review of alternatives—without as much debate as a new state song would engender—they endorse a substantial revision of the fundamental law of the land.

They have lost their grip on the enormity of what they are doing. And they have taken the wrong way out of a troublesome dilemma.

I am convinced that a constitutional amendment is a very poor solution to our current fiscal difficulties. It is unworkable, counterproductive, and even harmful. But it is not the caricature some critics suggest. It is a very serious proposal indeed. It deserves very serious review.

A mandated balance is not the only issue. There are many variations on the theme. Some propose a balanced budget statute. Others invent formulas to limit federal spending. Still others hope that Congress will produce an amendment for ratification by the states. All of these proposals are dangerous and poorly thought through. But the most alarming prospect of all is a new constitutional convention.

It's an uncharted course to an unknown destination. A balanced budget amendment is only one potential result. There are other popular crusades—to outlaw guns—to outlaw gun control—to make abortion a right—to make abortion a crime—to ban forced busing—to endow forced busing with a specific constitutional sanction.

Many passionate causes are deeply rooted in our nation. Many are well supported. Many are well financed. Many are eager to readjust the underpinnings of the United States of America.

At a constitutional convention, could the readjustments be limited? No one really knows. The Attorney General thinks so. The American Bar Association agrees. But there is only one precedent. And it is not a comforting one.

The only convention we've ever had was called to revise the Articles of Confederation. But the delegates didn't stop at revision. They scrapped the system. They built a new one. And what would prevent a wholesale recasting of the document *they* devised? Not the Constitution itself—it simply says that Congress "Shall call a convention for proposing amendments." And depriving the states of Senate representation is the only amendment specifically ruled out. Hopefully, the agenda *would* be limited.

If a runaway convention exceeded the limits thought to be imposed by those who convene it and three-fourths of the legislatures, responding to the kinds of popular pressures now being generated, were to ratify the result, who could say no?

How many of us are willing to gamble that our national

compass would not be disoriented? How many even perceive the risk?

There are too many questions here—and not enough answers.

We should not expose our Constitution to the prospect of substantial revision when there are other, less imposing alternatives. Neither should we trivialize it with money management schemes—particularly those which can do no good and a great deal of harm.

A mandated federal budget balance is just such an ill-considered contrivance. And it is largely the product of a basic misperception. The relationship between the deficit and the economy is a very close one indeed. But it is not a one-way affair. A bad budget can unbalance the economy. But a bad economy can also unbalance the budget. And no amendment could possibly cope with that.

When unemployment goes up only one percentage point —the deficit swells by some 20 billion dollars—20 billion dollars in lost tax revenues and increased social welfare costs—20 billion dollars drained from the federal purse without a single spending spree.

In times of severe recession, the impact on the budget can be devastating. We've had some recent experience.

In October, 1974, President Ford unwrapped his "Whip Inflation Now" Program. He pledged to hold the deficit to 9 billion dollars in fiscal 1975. But fate and recession intervened. Just three months later, the President revised that estimate to 35 billion dollars, and sent the Congress a fiscal 1976 recommendation for a 52 billion dollar deficit.

The men who made the WIN buttons lost their jobs— along with two million other Americans.

A year ago January, President Carter proposed a budget with a 60 billion dollar deficit. We worked hard to trim it—and by September, we had cut that deficit to 38 billion. But interest rates went up. Inflation pushed higher. And from September to January, the deficit increased by 5 billion dollars—when Congress wasn't even in session.

Constitutional amendments can't balance the economy. Resolutions passed in Richmond or Topeka can't dictate policy in Riyadh or Tehran. Decisions made in Washington's caucus rooms aren't always supported in the board rooms of New York.

Are we helpless then? Certainly not. Prudent fiscal management can work through the economy and lead us back to a steadier course. We are doing that job right now. But a suddenly imposed requirement for an immediate balance—or for one to be forged in the unknowable future—would have some very regrettable consequences.

Over the years, economists of nearly every persuasion have testified before our Committee. They have agreed on little more than this—you can't always catch a deficit with radical spending cuts and tax increases. That may only make it run faster.

For fiscal 1980, the President projects a 29 billion dollar deficit. But a 29 billion dollar spending cut would not bring the budget into balance. It would ripple through the economy with a tax revenue loss of many billions of dollars.

It would take a cut of at least 45 billion to put the books in balance. And that would cost more than a million American jobs. It might have an impact on inflation, but it would leave the economy far weaker than before. And where would we look for a cut of that magnitude?

Of course, a budget can be balanced by raising taxes as well as by cutting expenses. And some insist that closing loopholes would match our debits with credits.

In 1932, Herbert Hoover tried that. He rushed to balance the budget with a drastic hike in taxes. The rest is tragic history. Things got very much worse. Purchasing power had been drained from the economy exactly when it should have been injected.

Nineteen thirty-two was not a good year for the economy. Nineteen thirty-two was not a good year for Herbert Hoover.

But there is a third option. When the economy is growing, taxes rise faster than spending. And unless you enact a tax cut, increased spending never catches up with revenues. So you juice up spending. You stimulate inflation. You push people into higher brackets. Your tax revenues go up. And you point with pride at a balanced budget.

That is the stuff of conservatives' nightmares. And that is yet another way to meet a balanced budget mandate.

All of these potential consequences are unattractive indeed. But perhaps the very worst result would be a failure of flexibility in times of economic downturn. Economists of every respected school agree that increased federal spending or tax cuts producing a deficit may well be the only way to boost employment, generate investment, stimulate demand, accumulate capital, and prevent a downturn from deepening into a depression.

A mandated balance would blunt our sharpest fiscal tool. And that is why thoughtful advocates are quick to point to escape clauses.

But no escape clause could be framed quite cleverly enough. How would recession be defined? Who would announce its arrival? Who would be willing to lead the escape when the signs of a trend appeared. Would two-thirds of the Senate vote to abandon a constitutionally mandated balanced budget for a deficit unless the roof was caving in? Would we have time to pop the parachute before we hit the ground?

There are too many questions with no good answers— too many holes in the theory.

And so—some map a more sophisticated route to balance. They suggest that spending should be limited to a fixed percentage of GNP, or that growth in spending should be tied to GNP growth. But have they asked the right questions?

Our Constitution does only two things. It blueprints the structures by which we govern ourselves. And it defines the human rights we respect. Do we really want to devalue that currency with algebra and bar graphs?

We wouldn't even know where to begin the equation. Which magic number would we pick? To whose projections would we tie it? The President predicts a 3.2 percent GNP growth rate for 1980. But the Congressional Budget Office says 3.9 percent. This difference of seven-tenths percent in the growth of federal spending represents three and a half billion dollars.

Perhaps we should go to a prominent private sector forecaster. But Wharton Econometrics says 1.3 percent and Chase says 4.1.

It is sometimes proposed that the number be tied to last year's growth. But like generals preparing to fight the last war, politicians preparing to deal with last year's realities are poorly prepared indeed.

Should we be writing a guessing game into the Federal Constitution? Should we bind tomorrow's needs to yesterday's performance? How can we make good practical sense out of bad theoretical blueprints?

Too many questions with no good answers—too many holes in the theory.

Perhaps the most ironic twist is the role of the states in the budget balancing controversy. Twenty-five of them are leading us into a serious mistake. And they will pay the biggest price. If Congress must suddenly chop the deficit, it will land in the laps of the states. That is not a threat. It's a matter of arithmetic.

Where would the cuts be made? Where would we find that 45 billion dollars this year? Let me refer you to the charts we've prepared.

Our cities and states are drawing on Washington for every conceivable need—from the health and education of their children to the wages of the men who trim the statehouse lawn.

Over the last thirty years, federal grants-in-aid to state and local governments have grown five times faster than the gross national product.

In fiscal 1980, the average state expects to receive one billion, six hundred and fifty-nine million dollars from

Washington. The legislatures seem to be unaware of the consequences an overnight balance would bring.

During its 1975–76 session, the Pennsylvania legislature passed its call for a balanced federal budget. That was Resolution 236. Resolution 235 demanded a renewal of revenue sharing.

When the Oregon legislature passed its amendment resolution, a "whereas" clause suggested that "a balanced budget would lessen the need for increased state and local taxes." That's an odd theory—particularly in view of the fact that Oregon got one billion, seventy-five million dollars from Washington in fiscal 1978.

We could save 31 billion—2 billion more than the President's projected deficit—merely by killing revenue sharing, education grants, EPA sewage construction, community development block grants, and the CETA program.

Is that what they want in the legislatures? Do they think the Congress would slash its own perception of national needs before it touched the states'? And if we did exempt the states from surgery, what would be left to cut? Social security? National defense?

There is 82.9 billion dollars in the President's budget for grants to state and local governments. In 1978, the states ran a combined surplus of 29 billion—a figure that matches the President's deficit for fiscal 1980. An appealing solution to the balance dilemma leaps very quickly to mind.

It would be easy to ask, "Who's deficit is this?" and the states would not be pleased with the answer.

Of course, if we look to the states' example, we needn't make cuts at all. We can get into balance merely by following their long-standing and well accepted method of accounting. If we put capital investments in a separate accounting category, we'd have a much smaller deficit today. And it wouldn't make a jot of difference to our income, our outflow, or the state of the economy.

That is what the states do. That's what General Motors does. That is accepted practice.

It would also be easy to balance the budget by removing

various programs from it. The federal government already spends some 12 billion dollars through agencies that are not counted in the budget totals. More programs could be moved into the dark. Or, more use could be made of federal guarantees and similar devices.

The Budget Committee is determined to bring such programs under the budget's umbrella. Only then will we have a full, honest picture of real federal government activity. A balanced budget requirement would surely tempt the Congress to go the other way.

Creative accounting could provide us a meaningless paper balance, but is there any point in one? Is there any good reason for attaching a charade to the Constitution of our country?

The answers are clear. So are the holes in the theory.

We've been perfecting a different theory since 1975—a new congressional budget process. It was forged in reaction to 37 years of deficit spending in the 54 years between 1920 and 1974. It was established because that record was flatly unacceptable. And for the first time in its history, Congress took explicit steps to reverse that record of deficits.

For the first time in its history, Congress established a standing committee with one exclusive mission—to set a fiscal plan—to hold the Congress to it—to pull us back from those irresponsible deficits.

Contrary to the popular rhetoric, we have made tremendous progress. And ours is no simple task.

In the popular imagination, the budget resembles an hourglass, with assets and liabilities neatly stacked at opposite ends. If an imbalance develops, what could be simpler than tilting the glass until the sands even out?

But the budget is better compared to a watch. When it runs too fast or slow, a violent jolt may relieve frustration. But it will not repair a delicate mechanism. One has to determine which moving parts to lubricate—which gears to tighten—which counterweights to adjust.

We've been making those judgments. And the record is more impressive than rhetoric.

In our first year of 1975, recession prevailed—and George Meany demanded a hundred billion dollar deficit. We held it to 66 billion. And five years later, we are keeping the pressure on.

In 1975, the deficit was 3 percent of GNP. But in 1980, it is projected at 1.2 percent.

In 1980, the level of federal spending will be 30 billion dollars lower than it would have been if Washington took the same percentage of GNP as it did in 1975.

And during the four years of the congressional budget process, our spring budget resolutions have called for spending targets at an average of 28 billion dollars below the requests submitted by the authorizing committees.

That's not good enough. We can do better still. We intend to. And we already have all the statutes, formulas and amendments we need to get the job done. We are asking the right questions. We are sealing the holes in a workable, flexible theory. Why scrap a proven system for one that defies a working diagram? Why graft an irresponsible scheme to the fundamental law of the land?

As one Supreme Court justice said, our Constitution is not a rubber ball to be tossed about and played with by each succeeding child. It embodies the essence of our system. There is no room in it for yesterday's whim or tomorrow's fancy.

In the long run, that is the centrally important concern. But in the near term, there is nothing attractive about the federal deficit. This is not a pro-deficit Congress. I am not a pro-deficit Budget Chairman. This is not a pro-deficit speech. But we don't need fiscal handcuffs to wipe the deficit out. We need fiscal discipline. We need to make informed, prudent judgments about hundreds of separate spending choices. We need the will to make those judgments stick. If we have that will, no formula is necessary. If we don't, no formula will work.

INNOVATION vs. REGULATION

THE DAY INNOVATION DIED [1]

JOHN W. HANLEY [2]

"Our technological superiority is not mandated by heaven. Unless we pay close attention to it and invest in it, it will disappear" (W. Michael Blumenthal, Secretary of the Treasury).

Can the interests of the citizen be balanced against the interests of the business community? In a quest for a safe environment, has technological superiority been threatened? There are two sides to these questions. On one side, consumer groups have created powerful lobbies to oppose industrial change that seems to threaten the environment and health. On the other side, many businesses have argued that government red tape is burdensome and results in additional cost and delay in marketing.

Speaking to the point, John W. Hanley, president of Monsanto, a large chemical manufacturer, argues, "U.S. innovating has lagged far behind historical levels and this lag has been a major contributor to our present economic ills." Hanley addressed a luncheon meeting of the Men's Forum of the Houston Club, on September 26, 1978, a sympathetic audience of the leading citizens and businessmen of the community.

Criticism of government regulation often abounds in business circles such as this. Hanley, as a representative of industry, presents a typical causal analysis in which he argues that "a critical shortage of innovations (the effect) has resulted from the federal regulatory process" (the cause). He makes dramatic use of specific instances to prove his contentions. Like a good debater, he concludes with a specific plan.

The reader should compare the line of argument in this speech with the one delivered by Barbara Franklin, who presents the case of the government regulator.

Seeing many people here today with whom Monsanto has a business and professional relationship reinforces my

---

[1] Delivered to the Men's Forum, at the Texas Room of the Houston Club, Houston, Texas, 12 noon, September 26, 1978. Quoted by permission.
[2] For biographical note, see Appendix.

belief that we in St. Louis and you in Houston have a great deal in common.

Cynics might say, "Yes, both places are hotter than soup in the summer." They might add that our two baseball teams are not so hot.

But I shrug off those disrespectful comments and point to our mutual good sense in promoting an aggressive, diversified business community in our respective hometowns.

I applaud our mutual good taste in covering two of the world's greatest sports emporia—the Astrodome and Busch Stadium—with Monsanto's astroturf.

The fact that yours was the first commercial installation was a stroke of luck for both Monsanto and Houston. Monsanto got a catchy name for one of its new products. And Judge Roy Hofheinz, having discovered that grass wouldn't grow after the dome was painted, got a ready-made solution to his problem.

The Astros as well as other baseball and football teams might have played in the dirt for some time if Monsanto hadn't—a long time before the birth of the Astrodome—committed the necessary years of research and development to come up with synthetic playing surfaces. Industrial innovation takes time. It's not unusual, as you know, for a successful innovation to be a decade or longer in the making.

That brings me to the subject I'd like to review with you today—innovation—the status of innovation in the United States in 1978.

Assume for a moment that ten years ago *today* all US industrial innovation had stopped. Just imagine for a moment that September 26, 1968, was the day innovation died.

In the short run, we wouldn't have noticed much change. But today, life would be quite different.

Air transportation would not be so comfortable without jumbo or wide-body jets. Nor could pilots rely on the improved safety features that make flying in the US safer than going to a rock concert.

As for your health, the innovations that never were

would range from laser surgery to soft contact lenses, low-cholesterol egg substitutes, synthetic heart valves, and on and on.

Our families would forego the fire protection offered by inexpensive home smoke detectors. The term "home computer" would sound ridiculous, because computers would still be huge, expensive, difficult machines.

Even large businesses would find these computers less useful without today's improved data communications systems.

Of course, one might argue that those lost innovations would make little difference since we wouldn't know what we were missing.

But we could hardly miss the economic distress generated by the absence of innovation. Productivity gains would have all but disappeared while inflation and trade deficits climbed. More innovative nations would grab away our position as the world's technology leader. American jobs would be lost to more efficient foreign competitors. American stockholders and savers would see their holdings dwindle because of inflation and international devaluation of the dollar.

But wait a minute. Aren't we faced with all of those problems today? Well, you and the great majority of Americans know that, in fact, we are.

Obviously, innovation did not drop dead precisely ten years ago today. Yet a strong case can be made that, during that ten years, US innovation has lagged far behind historical levels. And this lag has been a major contributor to our present economic ills, which we cannot hope to alleviate unless we boost our innovation rate.

That's why I believe that our nation's most serious shortage today involves not energy or raw materials or jobs, but innovation.

This afternoon, I'd like to examine with you the evidence of what I regard as a critical shortage of innovation. I'll discuss how policies of the federal government contribute to the lag, and how overregulation can have an especially chilling effect on innovation. Finally, I will suggest a plan of action which I believe can help the nation out of this dilemma.

Innovation is a commodity that defies direct precise measurement—so we must resort to proxy measurements. Let me give you a few that indicate the dimensions of the problem.

—The nation's total research and development expenditures in constant dollars have declined by about 5 percent since the late sixties, while expenditures for *basic* research are down more than 10 percent.

—Industrial R and D spending since the late sixties has risen a little faster than inflation, but expenditures for *basic* research have declined more than 20 percent.

—R and D spending here has slipped from 3 percent of the gross national product in 1965 to about 2 percent a decade later, while Japan and West Germany have made substantial increases, and the Soviet Union has pushed well above 3 percent.

—Foreign inventors now receive about twice as many US patents each year as they did in 1968, while the number of foreign patents issued to American inventors has declined.

Granted, these are imperfect ways to gauge what's happening to innovation in this country, but they do point out that we're headed in the wrong direction. Furthermore, it's hard to ignore the indications that the very nature of industrial R and D is changing. Technical resources are being moved away from long-term basic research toward short-term improvements in existing products and processes.

Where does this lead? One example is suggested by an incident that happened in St. Louis just this summer. The board of directors of Eastern Airlines met in my city, which is headquarters for two major aircraft manufacturers. Frank Borman, the president of Eastern, defended his company's decision to purchase a fleet of French-made A-300 passenger jets.

Mr. Borman said: "What concerns me most is that US technology that once was the best in the world has not kept pace. The A-300 is here when we need it."

I'm sure that the business leaders of the southwest—especially here in the nation's energy capital—don't have to be convinced that innovation means growth and benefits for everyone. You see that all around you. In fact, where would the Sun Belt be today without a commercial innovation known as air conditioning?

A study by Data Resources Incorporated shows the broad economic benefits of innovation. Companies which are heavy R and D spenders, compared to all manufacturers, were found to increase employee productivity 75 percent faster while they raised prices only one-fifth as much. Furthermore, they created jobs 120 percent faster.

So it should concern every citizen when something happens that affects the innovation rate. The federal government—as ubiquitous as gravity—cannot help but affect innovation for better or worse at every turn.

Sensitive to this fact, the Carter administration has initiated a cabinet-level review of how federal policies affect innovation. Also, a subcommittee of the Senate Commerce, Science and Transportation Committee has begun exploring the connections among US trade deficits, federal policies, and industrial innovation.

There won't be any lack of areas to study. For instance, innovation requires venture capital which has been short since the bear market of 1974. In 1969, almost 700 small technology-oriented companies raised new capital in the nation's money markets. In 1975, only four such companies found public financing and last year it was still only 30. So the demands placed on capital markets in part by federal deficit spending cannot be ignored as a barrier to innovation.

Federal tax policies figure heavily in our country's output of innovation because they shape the overall investment climate. The US ranks far below other industrialized countries on percentage of national output reinvested in productive capacity. It's no coincidence that we also tax capital gains and stock dividends more harshly than most industrialized nations.

Federal antitrust laws create still another worry for innovators. Their new technology may be too successful and precipitate lawsuits.

But when it comes to frustrating would-be innovators, nothing beats the federal regulatory process. For starters, there is the staggering drain on financial resources. Economist Murray Weidenbaum, director of Washington University's Center for the Study of American Business, calculates that regulatory compliance will cost business almost $100 billion in 1979 alone.

Regulation injects new uncertainties into the already risky business of innovation.

Will regulatory approvals take so long that millions in sales will be lost—as well as the competitive lead?

Will the approval process cost so much that a useful innovation meant to serve a small market can never be profitable?

Will the fruits of innovation be lost entirely because of a needless product ban based on flimsy evidence?

These are not hypothetical situations. They can be demonstrated all too readily.

Take the pharmaceutical industry. Almost everyone will agree that we must proceed with proper caution on new drugs. But at what point should we begin asking who is looking after the public interest?

A pharmaceutical company in the US may wait one to four years for approval of a new drug application. Since it also takes several years to develop a modern drug, half the patent life may be gone before the product even reaches the marketplace. In fact, approval in the US generally lags so far behind other countries that American pharmaceutical companies have established manufacturing units abroad in part so as not to lose out on foreign sales.

The upshot is that jobs and capital in these instances are exported while fewer effective drugs are made available here. In the 15 years preceding 1962, there were 641 new drugs introduced in this country. But the next 15 years have produced only 247 new drugs.

A similar situation exists in the agricultural chemical industry. The fifties saw about 20 new pesticides enter the market. The sixties also produced about 20. But from 1971 to 1977, only three or four truly new products reached the market.

Monsanto's experience with its Roundup Herbicide tells the story well. Roundup was developed in 1970 after 15 years of research. Its unique chemistry destroys perennial weeds right down to the roots. Yet Roundup is about as toxic as table salt. It breaks down quickly in the soil, won't migrate to adjacent areas, and leaves no residue in the crops.

It was 1975 before Roundup received US regulatory approval for use with any major grain crops. Three years later, we're still waiting for approval for use with other crops. One of the ironies of this case is that regulation has slowed the introduction of a pesticide that is environmentally more attractive than many of those now on the market.

I doubt whether there is any more effective way to kill an innovative spirit than by scaring it to death. I can testify firsthand that a product ban based on flimsy evidence can do just that.

We at Monsanto were shocked when the federal government banned our *Cycle-safe* bottle for carbonated soft drinks. This plastic bottle, which took ten years to develop, first received regulatory approval in 1975. Shoppers in the test markets loved it because it was lightweight and shatter-resistant. And since it was recyclable and potentially refillable, it was an innovation that could help solve our nation's litter problem.

The raw materials for making *Cycle-safe* included a chemical called acrylonitrile. This has been used in food-contact applications for more than 30 years. But a 1977 study indicated that, in massive doses, it might cause cancer in rats.

Monsanto researchers, using the most sophisticated testing equipment available today, cannot find any trace of acrylonitrile leaching into the beverage under realistic conditions. But the regulators say that if the bottles were filled with acetic acid and stored for six months at 120 degrees fahrenheit, infinitesimal amounts of the chemical *could* leach into the solution. Never mind that a carbonated beverage stored at 120 degrees would burst the bottle in a few weeks—and that a child would have to drink 3,000 quarts of beverage every day for a year to equal the dose of acrylonitrile fed to the rats.

Despite the remoteness of the risk, the regulators chose to ignore the bottle's considerable real and potential benefits. The federal government said *Cycle-safe* must go.

Monsanto is still appealing that decision in the courts. I think we will win—long after the victory will have any value beyond establishing the principle that, without proper balancing of risks against benefits, such government decisions are foolish and capricious.

In the meantime, though, our three *Cycle-safe* plants have closed, eliminating nearly one thousand jobs. We have written off a good many millions of dollars, including $20 million worth of equipment and facilities.

This shock persuaded us—if we needed any further persuasion—that business cannot stand idle while regulatory agencies destroy innovative products without attempting to weigh the risks against the benefits. Thus, Monsanto has initiated a broad communications program through which we hope to bring a greater sense of balance to the national debate over industry regulation.

Not surprisingly, the *Cycle-safe* episode also helped turn more of Monsanto's R and D resources away from innovation and toward defense of other products.

Just yesterday in St. Louis, we dedicated a new $12 million toxicology laboratory where product safety testing will be done. In the past, we found it more economical to contract with outside laboratories for such testing. But today there aren't enough contract labs to handle all the toxicological testing needed to satisfy government regulations.

Monsanto is not alone in this. Another large chemical company reports that its spending for defensive research—research that will never produce any new knowledge or products—has gone up five times faster than spending for innovative research in recent years.

The Industrial Research Institute, an association of manufacturers with research facilities, surveyed its members and found an alarming rate of increase in the proportion of R and D spending that goes to meet regulatory requirements. Innovation will decline rapidly if this trend isn't changed.

Now please understand me: I am *not* calling for the elimination of regulation.

I am *not* disagreeing with the underlying social goals of protecting the consumer, the worker, and the environment.

But good sense must define a point of balance. We cannot go on ignoring the impact that government regulation is having on American innovation.

As Treasury Secretary Michael Blumenthal has said, "Our technological supremacy is not mandated by heaven."

What can we do, then, to safeguard our technological preeminence before it is too late? I would encourage every member of the Houston Club—and every American business leader—to seriously consider these three points for immediate action.

Point *one:* We must support the Carter administration's effort to learn how federal policies help or hinder industrial innovation—and to identify positive steps toward encouraging innovation.

The White House study, headed by Commerce Secretary Juanita Kreps, will include input from business and industry. This will be gathered through such groups as the Business Roundtable, the Conference Board, the Industrial Research Institute, and Ad Hoc Advisory Panels. If you are contacted for information, your views, or even a commitment of your time, I urge you to extend your fullest cooperation.

Point *two:* We must voice our concern about the innovation lag on Capitol Hill.

It's encouraging that Senators Howard Cannon and Adlai Stevenson of the Commerce, Science and Transportation Committee have shown interest. It's high time for the entire Congress to take notice.

Sharp illustrations of the problem drawn from your own business will get attention. Monsanto has tried this and found eager listeners. We've also suggested some specific legislative actions that I'd like to mention today.

One is an investment tax credit for industrial research and development expenditures. R and D is an investment in a productive future. Our tax laws should encourage large and small corporations to devote more resources to innovation.

We have also suggested that Congress establish a formal system of reviewing all regulatory agencies every three years. Congress should determine whether each agency is properly weighing the benefits of proposed regulations against the costs and the impact on industrial innovation.

Point *three:* We must take this issue to the people—to your associates and friends—because low public awareness decreases the likelihood of positive action in Washington.

The public is like Mrs. Einstein, when she was asked if she could make sense of her husband's theories.

"I understand the words," she said, "But I don't always understand the sentences."

Our task is to explain the sentences—to demonstrate that inflation, low productivity gains, trade deficits and lost jobs are all linked to innovation lag. We must carry this message to the public through grass-roots political action, through the news media, public speaking engagements, and personal contacts. Given the facts, the public can be depended on to reach sensible conclusions, and ultimately to influence the decision-makers in Washington.

Our nation is well-versed in the politics of energy, economy, environment, worker and consumer safety. Now we must give as much attention to the politics of innovation, because this will determine our ability to achieve all the other national goals.

American innovation has earned us the title of the greatest problem-solving society ever. This is not the time to relinquish that title. We must move quickly and decisively to reverse the innovation lag.

Ten years hence, we don't want to look back and say that *this* was the day innovation died.

CONSUMER SAFETY AND HEALTH [1]

Barbara Hackman Franklin [2]

Barbara H. Franklin, Commissioner of the Consumer Product Safety Commission, said: "The American people are saying they want less—but better—government. . . . It is sending seismic waves through the White House, the Congress and the agencies." President Carter has repeatedly emphasized his concern over simplifying the complexity of the federal regulatory structure; consequently he has launched a study of the rules of federal agencies by his Regulatory Council. The objectives of this effort are "to eliminate duplication and to uncover less costly ways of achieving health, safety and environmental goals" (John Dillon, *Christian Science Monitor*, March 1, 1979). Three agencies to come under scrutiny have been the Environmental Protection Agency (EPA), the Consumer Product Safety Commission (CPSC), and the Occupational Safety and Health Administration (OSHA).

Barbara H. Franklin, Commissioner of the Consumer Product Safety Commission, realized that she was on the spot when she addressed a "Conference for and about the Conspicuous Consumer" at 8:00 P.M., November 29, at the Hyatt Regency Hotel in Cambridge, Massachusetts. Under the sponsorship of Boston College, the conference attracted educators, consumerists, business leaders, and government officials.

Her main purpose was to defend the Consumer Product Safety Commission against the charge that it fosters unnecessary regulation and complicates the lives of the American people—or in her words that it is "a regulatory monster." It is interesting that Commissioner Franklin spent the first third of her time suggesting that she, like President Carter, recognized the need to simplify federal regulations. However, in the last two-thirds of the speech she shifted into an argument in favor of more effective regulation at less cost.

After establishing common ground with her listeners, the Commissioner turned her attention toward justifying the purpose of her agency: public health and safety. In her four-step plan, she

---

[1] Delivered at Conference for and about the Conspicuous Consumer, Boston College, Boston, Massachusetts, November 29, 1978. Quoted by permission.

[2] For biographical note, see Appendix.

reveals her aim when she says: "We need to rethink regulation—
to make it better, to make it work and to make it stick." She
planned her message with the consumer in mind—not those who
advocate less regulation. It is entirely possible that the Commissioner was interested in developing grass roots support for protecting her projected program against those who push for curtailing
of government activities in an important area.

As a federal regulator, I accept speaking engagements
these days with more and more trepidation. The trepidation turns to outright fear as the day of the speech arrives
and the experience of Winston Churchill comes to mind.

On one of his trans-Atlantic tours, a student asked, "Mr.
Churchill, doesn't it thrill you to know that every time you
make a speech the hall is packed to overflowing?"

Churchill pondered the question for a moment. Then
he replied, "Of course, it is flattering. But always remember
that if I were being hanged, the crowd would be twice as
big."

Churchill's point is not lost today. In view of predictions that government regulation is an idea whose time is
passing, the prospect of a public lynching is very intimidating—especially to a potential "lynchee."

I'll take my chances this evening. In fact, I welcome this
opportunity to discuss the issue of regulation with those of
you who ultimately will decide where it goes—consumers,
the business community, and government officials.

Across the country and across the political spectrum,
the American people are saying they want less—but better—
government.

The rallying cry is this: Government has gone overboard; overhaul the machinery, and stop the wasteful
spending. The specifics are more complex: a government
which fosters competition and social goals at a reasonable
cost; a government which is accessible and responsive, but
less intrusive and sluggish; a government more accountable
to the people, yet freer from the pressures of narrow special
interests.

It is a tall order.

It is sending seismic waves through the White House, the Congress, and the agencies.

And it is a bread and butter issue for every American.

The burden of regulation, once only a burning issue in business forums, today is on the tip of everyone's tongue. The message is being repeated in ways that graphically underscore the impact of regulation upon our basic economic health and social well-being:

—the direct costs to business, consumers, and the government.

—the indirect costs of business investments not made, plants not opened, job opportunities lost, reduced productivity, and new technologies dampened.

—the international costs, typified by the devalued dollar.

—the psychological costs of weakened leadership and the loss of consumer and taxpayer confidence.

In short, government is a dominant force in our lives. It is said to be the nation's biggest employer, its biggest consumer, and its biggest borrower. Government today exercises direct regulation over much of everything bought and sold in the US and indirect regulation over almost every other sector of the private economy. The now-defunct Commission on Federal Paperwork estimates that the total cost of federal paperwork is $100 billion a year—or about $500 per person. Already, *Newsweek* suggests that each year's harvest of administrative regulations is so large that it defies quantification.

Do we have a regulatory monster?

More and more people believe that we do and that it is long overdue for a leashing. The concern is fueled by the toll inflation is taking and an awakening of the press and the general public to what some businesspeople have been saying all along: that regulation, however intended to protect consumers and competitors from the marketplace abuses of a few, doesn't always work that way.

The critical issue is where we go from here and how.

Frankly, I am encouraged with the public demand for a better, more affordable government. It is too early to pinpoint precisely when results will emerge—but soon enough to predict that they will and that the impact had better be more substantive than symbolic.

For those of us in this room who have long been tilting at certain regulatory windmills, it is already heartening to feel the fresh winds of change.

I would be deluding you, however, if I did not admit to some concern, especially in the area of health and safety regulation.

I am a proponent of reform in this area, too—in order to better protect the public in a way business can live with, government can live with, and most of all, that the American people can live with. But in the current rush to give all government a bad rap, the great temptation is to forget why many important public health and safety programs exist.

The Consumer Product Safety Commission is a classic example.

One businessman put it this way: "Let's face it. CPSC is another federal agency that probably wouldn't be in existence if those of us in business had been doing our jobs properly."

He has a point.

The creation of the Commission was not an accident. It was born during the rising tide of consumerism, the first wave of product liability suits and legitimate concern about the safety of products consumers buy and use. It was said 20 million consumers were being injured each year—many needlessly, at an annual cost to the national economy of some $5.5 billion.

So Congress created the agency in 1973, giving us jurisdiction over the safety of some 10,000 consumer products.

Today, the familiar Washington formula—find a problem, pass a law, and set up a new agency—seems to be running out of steam. But make no mistake: public demand for a better quality of life has not.

A Harris public opinion poll this summer underscores the point.

Controlling crime, according to the survey, is seen as very important in improving the quality of life. So is better education, conserving energy, and curbing air and water pollution. More and more people emphasize safety in the workplace, and 74 percent place a high priority on making products and services safer, up almost ten percent over the last two years.

To me, the message of 1978 is this: CPSC, like other agencies whose job involves the public health and safety, has a responsibility to see that it happens—at a price that is reasonable.

In this spirit, I am recommending the Commission take four steps.

First, we must take a closer look at precisely when safety regulation makes sense, under what circumstances and to what extent.

In other words, we need to rethink safety regulation—to make it better, to make it work and to make it stick—in those cases where it is necessary.

In those instances where government intervention isn't needed, we should stay out. And in the vast majority of cases which fall somewhere between the two extremes, we must not hesitate to explore promising alternatives to regulation.

Personally, I'd like to see the Commission sign more agreements along the lines of the one we have with the Chain Saw Manufacturers Association. If a timely, effective standard addressing the safety of chain saws is written in the private sector, then everybody stands to benefit—the Commission, industry, and consumers.

Consumer education and information is another tool which too often is underestimated. The plain truth of the matter is that many, many accidents can be prevented only with changes in human behavior.

Second, the Commission should review its overall strategy to achieve greater consumer safety.

It may be that a vigorous campaign directed at top corporate managers is a wise expenditure of everybody's time and money. When the person at the top is tuned in to product safety, so is everyone else in the organization.

The Commission also should convene regional conferences so that companies can learn, firsthand, what others are doing to make and sell safer products, the organizational mechanisms they've put in place, and the procedures they follow to get defective products off the production line, off retail shelves, and out of consumers' hands.

Then, too, the Commission must find, in the very near future, special ways to work with small businesses—those companies who lack the time and resources to deal with every finite detail of regulation. A major first step would be to assure that the concerns of small companies are reflected in our regulatory decision-making early in the process.

Third, we must reduce unnecessary delay.

Frankly, as many representatives of companies as consumer groups complain whenever our work becomes unduly protracted. Predictability in public policy is thwarted. The ability for businesspeople to plan ahead is stymied. Protection for consumers can be denied. Scarce resources, public and private, are squandered.

An issue coming before the Commission next month is a vivid case in point.

The Commission now is in its fifth year of developing a mandatory safety standard for power mowers—five years in which consumers have received no uniform protection from some hazards which the agency, a major trade association, and a national consumer group agree exist.

The fault, in my judgment, rests heavily on the Commission's shoulders. Only this summer did we decide to stagger consideration of the complex problems—in order to reduce the burden on industry and to try to hasten the day when consumers could receive some protection.

Other factors, however, also contributed to the delay, not the least of which is an expensive publicity campaign waged by the industry to discredit the proposal almost from the moment it was drafted.

All in all, the years invested in the project have taken quite a toll, literally and figuratively. Surely it was in everybody's best interests to find a better way to protect consumers.

Fourth, cost/benefit analysis.

Let's say it right up front: Product safety costs, and somebody's got to pay.

That "somebody" is called the consumer or the taxpayer —depending who passes along the costs, business or government. Then, too, if an accident occurs, the consumer and his or her family get it in the pocketbook in another way. There are staggering medical and hospital bills, lost income, higher insurance rates—to say nothing of the extensive pain, suffering, and possible loss of life.

In my judgment, the Commission needs to get a better handle on issues like these.

Already, by law, we are required to establish the need for and general impact of our regulations. But more is needed. Indeed, the courts seem to agree—if we expect our proposals to withstand judicial scrutiny. So does President Carter. He is urging a hard look at the goals, benefits, and costs of all regulatory proposals, adding that he wants the "consumer protected . . . with the least adverse inflationary effect."

Addressing safety issues in the cost/benefit context is not a panacea. Precise determination of the benefits and burdens is difficult, especially in the area of health and safety regulation. Our present ability to consider the full range of costs is elementary. On the benefit side of the equation, it is downright primitive.

But even with what we know now the cost/benefit way

of thinking is useful. It sets up a real-life framework for regulators to ask the hard questions, make the tradeoff's, and set priorities.

I believe this is what the American people expect from their government. Indeed, the majority of Americans, according to a new study by Cambridge Reports, Inc., want the benefits and burdens considered and the tough tradeoff's made.

All of us share the same goals—economic well-being and a healthy, safer environment in which to live. But to reach these goals, we must use our resources well, trying to obtain the most benefit and leverage for every dollar—public and private—we spend.

When it comes to consumer safety and health, my own feeling is that in certain circumstances, government does need to step in. On the other hand, optimal protection of the public requires vigorous attention to safety factors long before products reach the store shelves or the hands of consumers. Thus, the onus really is on business. Putting it another way, the point is this: it's wiser and cheaper to design and sell safer products or to locate and correct defects early on than to be the defendant in product liability suits, mount expensive recall campaigns and endure the sales-wrecking publicity and weakening of consumer confidence.

The challenge to all of us—and I believe, the opportunity—is to make America work better again.

When I say "better" I do not mean a bigger government which crowds out the private sector or the individual.

I do not mean a more meddlesome government, burrowing deeper into the affairs of business "to fix things that ain't broke."

But I also do not believe that we can turn back the clock, championing only those solutions which fit other times in our national life 50, 30, or even 20 years ago.

We must learn from our mistakes of the past—so that we can do better in the future. Our country was not built by complacency or excessive caution, but by boldness, innovation, and competition.

Now it is up to us to carry on in the same spirit. Where we go from here really is up to us.

AN ELOQUENT MOMENT

ANNOUNCING THE CAMP DAVID ACCORDS [1]

Jimmy Carter, Anwar el-Sadat, and Menachem Begin [2]

In a broad context, Donald C. Bryant, a prominent speech specialist, describes eloquence as "an attribute of a person, of an occasion; sometimes a quality of language, a genre of discourse." Eloquence in language indeed has become a rare quality because it is utilitarian concerns—such as getting high ratings in opinion polls—that motivate public figures, rather than a desire to touch listeners deeply by uttering memorable statements. In a classical sense, the word eloquence has almost disappeared from current usage. But at rare times, even today, we are treated to what we can characterize as eloquent.

On September 17, 1978, television viewers were witness to such an event. Seated at a table before the cameras in the East Room of the White House (10:30 P.M.), President Jimmy Carter, President Anwar el-Sadat of Egypt, and Prime Minister Menachem Begin of Israel elaborated on the completion of the historic "Framework for Peace in the Middle East" and a "Framework for the Conclusion of a Peace Treaty Between Egypt and Israel." These accords, the results of thirteen long, hard days of negotiations at nearby Camp David in Maryland, were in the words of *Newsweek* "a giant step toward peace" (September 25, 1978, p 76). Senator Frank Church, chairman of the Senate Foreign Relations Committee, said, "The Camp David Accords must surely be accounted one of the most remarkable achievements of modern diplomatic history (from speech delivered February 18, 1978, at the 71st Annual Award Dinner of Bnai Zion).

Although the occasion was memorable, the brief speeches, were little more than progress reports and expressions of friendship. They were no longer than about fifteen minutes in all, and preceded the actual signing of the treaties. President Sadat, from manuscript, and Prime Minister Begin, extemporaneously, expressed gratitude to their host and lauded the peace settlement. With pleasant informality and sincerity, Begin spoke the longest and was most moving. It was obvious that in attempting to find

---

[1] Delivered at 10:30 P.M., September 17, 1978, East Wing of White House, Washington, D.C.

[2] For biographical note, see Appendix.

answers to complex international problems, the three men had developed respect for one another in the course of their humanitarian endeavors and they conveyed to their viewers a sense of empathy and rapport. The whole scene was eloquent, as the three national leaders, from divergent cultures, responding to the drama of the moment, inspired their worldwide audience with faith and hope.

In recognition of their achievements, Begin and Sadat were awarded the Nobel Peace Prize.

A sequel to the accords was the signing of the Egyptian-Israeli Peace Treaty at the White House on March 26, 1979, when the three men again spoke.

JIMMY CARTER

When we first arrived at Camp David, the first thing upon which we agreed was to ask the people of the world to pray that our negotiations would be successful. Those prayers have been answered far beyond any expectations. We are privileged to witness tonight a significant achievement in the cause of peace, an achievement none thought possible a year ago, or even a month ago, an achievement that reflects the courage and wisdom of these two leaders.

Through 13 long days at Camp David, we have seen them display determination and vision and flexibility which was needed to make this agreement come to pass. All of us owe them our gratitude and respect. They know that they will always have my personal admiration.

There are still great difficulties that remain and many hard issues to be settled. The questions that have brought warfare and bitterness to the Middle East for the last 30 years will not be settled overnight. But we should all recognize the substantial achievements that have been made.

One of the agreements that President Sadat and Prime Minister Begin are signing tonight is entitled "A Framework For Peace in the Middle East."

This framework concerns the principles and some specifics, in the most substantive way, which will govern a comprehensive peace settlement. It deals specifically with the future of the West Bank and Gaza and the need to resolve the Palestinian problem in all its aspects. The framework document proposes a five-year transitional period in the West Bank and Gaza during which the Israeli military government will be withdrawn and a self-governing authority will be elected with full autonomy. It also provides for Israeli forces to remain in specified locations during this period to protect Israel's security.

The Palestinians will have the right to participate in the determination of their own future, in negotiations which will resolve the final status of the West Bank and Gaza, and then to produce an Israeli-Jordanian peace treaty.

These negotiations will be based on all the provisions and all the principles of United Nations Security Council Resolution 242. And it provides that Israel may live in peace, within secure and recognized borders. And this great aspiration of Israel has been certified without constraint, with the greatest degree of enthusiasm, by President Sadat, the leader of one of the greatest nations on Earth.

The other document is entitled, "Framework For the Conclusion of a Peace Treaty Between Egypt and Israel."

It provides for the full exercise of Egyptian sovereignty over the Sinai. It calls for the full withdrawal of Israeli forces from the Sinai and, after an interim withdrawal which will be accomplished very quickly, the establishment of normal, peaceful relations between the two countries, including diplomatic relations.

Together with accompanying letters, which we will make public tomorrow, these two Camp David agreements provide the basis for progress and peace throughout the Middle East.

There is one issue on which agreement has not been reached. Egypt states that the agreement to remove Israeli settlements from Egyptian territory is a prerequisite to a peace treaty. Israel states that the issue of the Israeli settlements should be resolved during the peace negotiations. That's a substantial difference. Within the next two weeks, the Knesset will decide on the issue of these settlements.

Tomorrow night, I will go before the Congress to explain these agreements more fully and to talk about their implications for the United States and for the world. For the moment, and in closing, I want to speak more personally about my admiration for all of those who have taken part in this process and my hope that the promise of this moment will be fulfilled.

During the last two weeks, the members of all three delegations have spent endless hours, day and night, talking, negotiating, grappling with problems that have divided their people for 30 years. Whenever there was a danger that human energy would fail, or patience would be exhausted or good will would run out—and there were many such moments—these two leaders and the able advisers in all delegations found the resources within them to keep the chances for peace alive.

Well, the long days at Camp David are over. But many months of difficult negotiations still lie ahead. I hope that the foresight and the wisdom that have made this session a success will guide these leaders and the leaders of all nations as they continue the progress toward peace.

Thank you very much.

ANWAR EL-SADAT

Dear President Carter, in this historic moment, I would like to express to you my heartfelt congratulations and appreciation. For long days and nights, you devoted your time and energy to the pursuit of peace. You have been most courageous when you took the gigantic step of convening this meeting. The challenge was great and the risks were high, but so was your determination. You made a commitment to be a full partner in the peace process. I'm happy to say that you have honored your commitment.

The signing of the framework for the comprehensive peace settlement has a significance far beyond the event. It signals the emergence of a new peace initiative, with the American nation in the heart of the entire process.

In the weeks ahead, important decisions have to be made if we are to proceed on the road to peace. We have to reaffirm the faith of the Palestinian people in the ideal of peace.

The continuation of your active role is indispensable. We need your help and the support of the American people. Let me seize this opportunity to thank each and every American for his genuine interest in the cause of people in the Middle East.

Dear friend, we came to Camp David with all the good will and faith we possessed, and we left Camp David a few minutes ago with a renewed sense of hope and inspiration. We are looking forward to the days ahead with an added determination to pursue the noble goal of peace.

Your able assistants spared no effort to bring out this happy conclusion. We appreciate their spirit and dedication. Our hosts at Camp David and the State of Maryland were most generous and hospitable. To each one of them and to all those who are watching this great event, I say thank you.

Let us join in a prayer to God Almighty to guide our path. Let us pledge to make the spirit of Camp David a new chapter in the history of our nations.

Thank you, Mr. President.

MENACHEM BEGIN

Mr. President of the United States, Mr. President of the Arab Republic of Egypt, ladies and gentlemen:

The Camp David conference should be renamed. It was the Jimmy Carter conference.

The President undertook an initiative most imaginative in our time and brought President Sadat and myself and our colleagues and friends and advisers together under one roof. In itself, it was a great achievement. But the President took a great risk for himself and did it with great civil courage. And it was a famous French field commander who

said that it is much more difficult to show civil courage
than military courage.

And the President worked. As far as my historic experience is concerned, I think that he worked harder than our
forefathers did in Egypt building the pyramids.

Yes, indeed, he worked day and night, and so did we.

PRESIDENT CARTER: Amen.

PRIME MINISTER BEGIN: Day and night. We used to go
to bed at Camp David between 3 and 4 o'clock in the
morning, arise, as we are used to since our boyhood, between 5 and 6, and continue working.

The President showed interest in every section, every
paragraph, every sentence, every word, every letter—of the
framework agreements.

We had some difficult moments—as usually there are
some crises in negotiations, as usually somebody gives a hint
that perhaps he would like to pick up and go home. It's
all usual. But ultimately, ladies and gentlemen, the President of the United States won the day. And peace now
celebrates a great victory for the nations of Egypt and
Israel and for all mankind.

Mr. President, we, the Israelis, thank you from the
bottom of our hearts for all you have done for the sake of
peace, for which we prayed and yearned more than 30
years. The Jewish people suffered much, too much. And,
therefore, peace to us is a striving, coming innermost from
our heart and soul.

Now, when I came here to the Camp David conference,
I said, perhaps as a result of our work, one day people
will, in every corner of the world, be able to say, *Habemus
pacem,* in the spirit of these days. Can we say so tonight?
Not yet. We still have to go a road until my friend President
Sadat and I sign the peace treaties.

We promised each other that we shall do so within three
months. Mr. President [*referring to President Sadat*], tonight, at this celebration of the great historic event, let us
promise each other that we shall do it earlier than within
three months.

Mr. President, you inscribed your name forever in the history of two ancient civilized peoples, the people of Egypt and the people of Israel. Thank you, Mr. President.

PRESIDENT CARTER: Thank you very much.

PRIME MINISTER BEGIN: Oh, no, no, no. I would like to say a few words about my friend, President Sadat. We met for the first time in our lives last November in Jerusalem. He came to us as a guest, a former enemy, and during our first meeting we became friends.

In the Jewish teachings, there is a tradition that the greatest achievement of a human being is to turn his enemy into a friend, and this we do in reciprocity. Since then, we had some difficult days. I'm not going now to tell you the saga of those days. Everything belongs to the past. Today, I visited President Sadat in his cabin, because in Camp David you don't have houses, you only have cabins. And he then came to visit me. We shook hands. And, thank God, we again could have said to each other, "You are my friend."

And, indeed, we shall go on working in understanding, and in friendship, and with good will. We will still have problems to solve. Camp David proved that any problem can be solved if there is good will and understanding and some, *some* wisdom.

May I thank my own colleagues and friends, the Foreign Minister, the Defense Minister, Professor Barak, who was the Attorney General—and now he is going to be His Honor, the Justice of the Supreme Court, the Israeli Brandeis—and Dr. Rosenne, and our wonderful Ambassador to the United States, Mr. Simcha Dinitz, and all our friends, because without them that achievement wouldn't have been possible.

I express my thanks to all the members of the American delegation, headed by the Secretary of State, a man whom we love and respect. And so, I express my thanks to all the members of the Egyptian delegation who worked so hard together with us, headed by Deputy Prime Minister, Mr.

Touhamy, for all they have done to achieve this moment. It is a great moment in the history of our nations and, indeed, of mankind.

I looked for a precedent; I didn't find it. It was a unique conference, perhaps one of the most important since the Vienna Conference in the nineteenth century; perhaps.

And now, ladies and gentlemen, allow me to turn to my own people from the White House in my own native tongue.

[At this point, the Prime Minister spoke briefly in Hebrew.]

Thank you, ladies and gentlemen.

FOREIGN COMMITMENTS

OUR CHINA POLICY IN A WIDER CONTEXT [1]

Zbigniew Brzezinski [2]

Formal recognition of the People's Republic of China, January 1, 1979, was one of the biggest stories and most significant developments in American foreign relations of the year. The announcement brought a number of protests over the changing diplomatic posture with Taiwan. Senator Barry Goldwater called the accord "a cowardly act" that "stabs in the back the nation of Taiwan." William Loeb, publisher of the right-wing Manchester (New Hampshire) *Union Leader,* editorialized "When a nation sells out its ally for a price, it earns mistrust. When it sells out its ally for nothing, it earns contempt." Obviously wishing to set the record straight and counter the negative reactions, the administration attempted to clear the air by explaining exactly what US recognition of the People's Republic entailed.

On January 15, 1979, a briefing session was held at the State Department for 500 business leaders. The administration's position was presented by Secretary of State Cyrus R. Vance, Secretary of the Treasury W. Michael Blumenthal, Secretary of Commerce Juanita M. Kreps, and Presidential Adviser Zbigniew Brzezinski (his formal title is Assistant to the President for National Security Affairs). Each one spoke briefly to the gathering.

Reproduced here is a clear enunciation of US foreign policy by Dr. Brzezinski, who had played a key role in normalizing relations with the People's Republic of China. His terse and well-organized presentation also gives a realistic overview of the wider context of international developments at the time. Some reporters suggested that Vance and Brzezinski were at variance on effects of the China tie, particularly as it might influence Russian relations (see Bernard Gwertzman, New York *Times,* January 16, 1979). A more accurate interpretation probably is that their positions were not really that far apart. Secretary Vance asserted that the United States was moving toward its objective "of maintaining a stable equalibrium among United States, Japan, China and

---

[1] Delivered to members of the National Council for US/China Trade and the USA/ROC Economic Council, January 15, 1979, State Department, Washington, D.C. Title supplied by editor.

[2] For biographical note, see Appendix.

the Soviet Union." Hard-hitting and concerned about global co-operation and not just about the Russian position, Brzezinski stated, "Few actions will contribute more to the security and stability of our important positions around the rim of Asia . . . than a constructive involvement with China. As we improve our relations with Peking, China will also wish to keep us involved in the region and not, as in the past, seek to drive us away."

My purpose is to place our China policy in a wider context.

As I address you, a number of troubling developments dominate the headlines:

—The Shah of Iran . . . [left] for a rest, leaving behind him a new administration which will seek to return tranquility to an unsettled country in which the United States has an enormous stake.

—Vietnam has invaded its neighbor, Cambodia. Through an act of aggression, it has imposed a subservient regime upon a Cambodian people wearied of the inhumane, callous rule of Pol Pot.

—Among the first governments to recognize the new Vietnamese-installed regime in Phnom Penh was Afghanistan, a strategically important country which borders on Iran and Pakistan and in which Soviet influence has increased significantly in recent months.

—The situation in the Horn of Africa and in South Yemen, Angola, and southern Africa remains uncertain, as Cuban troops continue to promote Soviet interests.

—Indeed, all the developing countries in the arc from northeast Asia to southern Africa continue to search for viable forms of government capable of managing the process of modernization. Their instability, uncertainty, and weakness can be exploited and intensified by outside powers.

Balanced against these unsettling developments, however, are a number of quieter yet more significant, positive developments:

—Progress has been made in bringing peace to the Middle East. The progress is slow and often painful. But through the persistent diplomacy of President Carter and Secretary Vance, we are, I believe, inexorably moving toward the realization of the Camp David accords. We are promoting reconciliation to one of the most volatile disputes in the world.

—In Latin America, United States policy has undergone significant change and our relations with most countries in the region are at or near all time highs. The ratification of the Panama Canal treaties was an historical milestone.

—We have significantly improved the nature of our relations with black African countries.

—Our relations with India have never been better; and we are retaining our ties of friendship with Pakistan.

—In East Asia, a delicate balance of power exists favorable to our interests. We have normalized relations with China, in part, to consolidate the balance.

—Such regional organizations as ASEAN [Association of Southeast Asian Nations] and OAU [Organization for African Unity] are playing an increasingly positive role in bringing stability to their regions.

—In recognition of the growing conventional military capability of the Soviet Union, we are increasing our military expenditures, as are our NATO allies, to make sure our European defenses remain strong.

—While we have not yet managed to establish a more stable world monetary and trading system, we have made progress in recent months in stabilizing the dollar and in creating a more orderly and growing world market through MTN.

—We will reach a SALT II agreement which will place a cap on the deployment of new and more missiles and which introduces a note of stability in the precarious strategic balance between the Soviet Union and the United States.

Added to these favorable developments are those of the spirit. After the debilitating decade of Vietnam and Watergate, our people are returning to their social moorings and exhibiting their traditional will and idealism. Worldwide, too, we have once again assumed the mantle of moral leadership, with the importance we attach to human rights, nuclear non-proliferation, and limitation of conventional arms sales. Certainly as much as and probably more than any other major power, the United States is addressing in a forthright manner the problems of our age. We remain an innovative society and a worldwide source of inspiration.

These positive developments are the result of the President's commitment—as he enunciated at Notre Dame more than a year ago—to a policy of constructive global engagement, a policy of trying to influence the changes of our era in directions that are compatible with our interests and values. Under that broad heading, we have crystallized seven fundamental objectives for our foreign policy:

First, to enhance our military security;

Second, to reinforce our ties with our key allies and promote a more cooperative world system;

Third, to respond in a positive way to the economic and moral challenge of the so-called North-South relationship;

Fourth, to improve relations between East and West;

Fifth, to help resolve the more threatening regional conflicts and tensions;

Sixth, to cope with such emerging global issues as nuclear proliferation and arms dissemination;

And *finally,* to reassert traditional American values—especially human rights.

At the outset, I should note that American foreign policy confronts a fundamental analytical question: Are the issues of the moment which I mentioned earlier—Iran, Indochina, the Horn, Afghanistan—indications of longer term trends? Do we respond to these issues not only with the sense of urgency which is obviously called for, but with a sense of historical despair as well? Or are the positive developments more indicative of our era? Should we continue on course?

In short, is an optimistic or pessimistic view of history justified? It seems to me that this issue underlies the emerging foreign policy debate in the United States.

Without being pollyannaish, this administration is basically optimistic. We recognize the future is ours only with effort. Continued American vigilance, preparedness, and decisiveness are necessary to grasp the better future before us. But an optimistic view of history and of America's future lies at the heart of this administration's foreign policy and of our China policy.

I do not mean to downplay or belittle the seriousness of the current foreign policy challenges. Important, indeed vital, issues are at stake. But in each situation, we are developing responses appropriate to the challenges involved. The United States will suffer occasional setbacks, but we will continue to be able to offset our losses with gains elsewhere—such as those that have occurred in recent years in our relations with India, Egypt, Eastern Europe, Ghana, the Sudan, and East Asia.

What we emphatically reject are apocalyptic visions about the future ability of the United States to pursue and defend our interests abroad. The pessimism that one hears from many quarters conveys a sense of Armageddon and of the need to rush to the barricade at every challenge without forethought.

Today, we seek neither a world order based on a Pax Americana, nor an order based on a Soviet-American condominium. Neither order is possible or just.

Rather, we are in the process of creating a diverse and stable community of independent states. Working with our traditional allies, for we cannot do the job alone, we are beginning to create a framework for wide-ranging international cooperation involving the United States, Western Europe, Japan, and many of the emerging regional powers such as Mexico, Venezuela, Brazil, Nigeria, Saudi Arabia, India, and Indonesia. And with the establishment of full diplomatic relations with the People's Republic of China, we very significantly increase the scope of international cooperation.

We wish, of course, to include the Soviet Union in that framework of cooperation. Indeed, a fundamental choice the Soviet Union faces is whether to become a responsible partner in the creation of a global system of genuinely independent states or whether to exclude itself from global trends and derive its security exclusively from its military might and its domination of a few clients. We hope and encourage the Soviet Union to be cooperative, but, whichever path the Soviet Union chooses, we will continue our efforts to shape a framework for global cooperation based not on domination but on respect for diversity.

We recognize that the world is changing under the influence of forces no government can control. The world's population is experiencing a political awakening on a scale without precedent in its history. The global system is undergoing a significant redistribution of political and economic power.

The record of the past two years suggests, however, that the United States need not fear this change. To the contrary, the record shows that we can shape this change to our benefit and attain security in a world of diversity.

Not only does the record of the past two years suggest realistic optimism is warranted. Our own past and the quality of our people also encourage confidence. For, our national experience as a nation of diverse origins and of change speaks to the emerging global condition. Not just our wealth, not just our military might, but our history as a pluralistic people and our commitment to the values of freedom and independence which now stir all of mankind give us a naturally key role in shaping the trends of our time.

Given our assessment of history and the goals of the administration, these points should be made about our China policy:

—We see normalization as having long-term, historic significance. It comprises part of our effort to consolidate and improve our relations with all the emerging powers in the world. And none of these powers is more important than China, with its nearly billion people and third largest defense budget in the world.

—We did not normalize out of tactical or expedient considerations. Rather we recognized reality. The People's Republic of China is going to play an increasing role in world affairs, and it was important for us to have a continuing, broadened, and structured relationship with this government.

—We recognize that the PRC and we have different ideologies and economic and political systems. We recognize that to transcend the differences and to make our new relationship successful will require patience, wisdom, and understanding. We harbor neither the hope, nor the desire, that through extensive contacts with China we can remake that nation into the American image.

—Indeed, we accept our differences. Normalization is an important part of our global effort to create a stable community of diverse and independent nations. As President Carter stated in his cable to Premier Hua Kuo-feng on January 1, "The United States desires a world of diversity in which each nation is free to make a distinctive contribution . . . to the manifold aspirations . . . of mankind. We welcome the growing involvement of the People's Republic of China in world affairs."

—We consider China as a key force for global peace simply by being China: an independent and strong nation reaching for increased contact with the rest of the world while remaining basically self-reliant and resistant of any efforts by others to dominate it.

—As Vice President Mondale stated, "We feel bonds of friendship, but sentiment alone cannot bridge the gap between us. What has brought us together is an awareness of our parallel interests in creating a world of economic progress, stability, and peace."

The community of interest we share with China is particularly evident in Asia, where we both desire peace, stability, and nations free of outside domination.

East, Southeast, and South Asia is one of the most important regions of the world today. The economies of the area are booming; the people are dynamic. The United States has great economic and security interests around the rim of Asia: In Japan, South Korea, all the Pacific islands down to the Philippines, and in Southeast Asia as well.

To protect our interests, we retain a strong military presence in the region, we maintain appropriate weapon sales throughout the region, and we are prepared to act on our interests should the need arise.

Few actions will contribute more to the security and stability of our important positions around the rim of Asia, however, than a constructive involvement with China. As we improve our relations with Peking, China will also wish to keep us involved in the region and not, as in the past, seek to drive us away.

For the first time in decades, we can enjoy simultaneously good relations with both China and Japan. It is difficult to overstress the importance of this fact. Normalization consolidates a favorable balance of power in the Far East and enhances the security of our friends.

Now the Chinese are turning outward and extending their hand to the West. We are prepared to respond less in confidence that in the future their hand will remain extended than in the knowledge that without a reciprocal gesture, their hand would certainly be withdrawn. And by developing bonds of commerce and shared understanding, we reduce the chances of future animosity.

That is why we have completed the process of normalization begun by President Nixon, President Ford, and Secretary Kissinger.

Normalization therefore is an act rooted in historical optimism and political realism. This change in our China policy does not represent retreat or abandonment of our previous positions. Rather, it reflects our determination to be globally engaged, to welcome diversity, and to shape our future.

For a generation, we said "No" to the reality of East Asia. We refused to recognize reality, we sought to isolate China, and we lived by myths—with two wars and with incalculable cost to the region and to us.

Now, we say "Yes" to reality. We are confident that as an Asian and Pacific power with a positive relationship with Peking, we will significantly contribute to the peace and prosperity of the American people and of all peoples in the region.

developing bonds of commerce and shared understanding, we reduce the chances of future animosity.

That is why we have completed the process of normalization begun by President Nixon, President Ford, and Secretary Kissinger.

Normalization therefore is an act rooted in historical optimism and political realism. This change in our China policy does not represent retreat or abandonment of our previous positions. Rather, it reflects our determination to be globally engaged, to welcome diversity, and to shape our future.

For a generation, we said "No" to the reality of East Asia. We refused to recognize reality, we sought to isolate China, and we lived by myths—with two wars and with incalculable cost to the region and to us.

Now, we say "Yes" to reality. We are confident that as an Asian and Pacific power with a positive relationship with Peking, we will significantly contribute to the peace and prosperity of the American people and of all peoples in the region.

beginning to create a framework for wide-ranging international cooperation involving the United States, Western Europe, Japan, and many of the emerging regional powers such as Mexico, Venezuela, Brazil, Nigeria, Saudi Arabia, India, and Indonesia. And with the establishment of full diplomatic relations with the People's Republic of China, we very significantly increase the scope of international cooperation.

We wish, of course, to include the Soviet Union in that framework of cooperation. Indeed, a fundamental choice the Soviet Union faces is whether to become a responsible partner in the creation of a global system of genuinely independent states or whether to exclude itself from global trends and derive its security exclusively from its military might and its domination of a few clients. We hope and encourage the Soviet Union to be cooperative, but, whichever path the Soviet Union chooses, we will continue our efforts to shape a framework for global cooperation based not on domination but on respect for diversity.

We recognize that the world is changing under the influence of forces no government can control. The world's population is experiencing a political awakening on a scale without precedent in its history. The global system is undergoing a significant redistribution of political and economic power.

The record of the past two years suggests, however, that the United States need not fear this change. To the contrary, the record shows that we can shape this change to our benefit and attain security in a world of diversity.

Not only does the record of the past two years suggest realistic optimism is warranted. Our own past and the quality of our people also encourage confidence. For, our national experience as a nation of diverse origins and of change speaks to the emerging global condition. Not just our wealth, not just our military might, but our history as a pluralistic people and our commitment to the values of freedom and independence which now stir all of mankind give us a naturally key role in shaping the trends of our time.

Given our assessment of history and the goals of the administration, these points should be made about our China policy:

—We see normalization as having long-term, historic significance. It comprises part of our effort to consolidate and improve our relations with all the emerging powers in the world. And none of these powers is more important than China, with its nearly billion people and third largest defense budget in the world.

—We did not normalize out of tactical or expedient considerations. Rather we recognized reality. The People's Republic of China is going to play an increasing role in world affairs, and it was important for us to have a continuing, broadened, and structured relationship with this government.

—We recognize that the PRC and we have different ideologies and economic and political systems. We recognize that to transcend the differences and to make our new relationship successful will require patience, wisdom, and understanding. We harbor neither the hope, nor the desire, that through extensive contacts with China we can remake that nation into the American image.

—Indeed, we accept our differences. Normalization is an important part of our global effort to create a stable community of diverse and independent nations. As President Carter stated in his cable to Premier Hua Kuo-feng on January 1, "The United States desires a world of diversity in which each nation is free to make a distinctive contribution . . . to the manifold aspirations . . . of mankind. We welcome the growing involvement of the People's Republic of China in world affairs."

—We consider China as a key force for global peace simply by being China: an independent and strong nation reaching for increased contact with the rest of the world while remaining basically self-reliant and resistant efforts by others to dominate it.

—As Vice President Mondale stated, "We feel b friendship, but sentiment alone cannot bridge the tween us. What has brought us together is an awar our parallel interests in creating a world of econom ress, stability, and peace."

The community of interest we share with Chin ticularly evident in Asia, where we both desire pe bility, and nations free of outside domination.

East, Southeast, and South Asia is one of the r portant regions of the world today. The economie area are booming; the people are dynamic. The States has great economic and security interests arc rim of Asia: In Japan, South Korea, all the Pacifi down to the Philippines, and in Southeast Asia as

To protect our interests, we retain a strong presence in the region, we maintain appropriate sales throughout the region, and we are prepared t our interests should the need arise.

Few actions will contribute more to the secu stability of our important positions around the rim however, than a constructive involvement with C we improve our relations with Peking, China will a to keep us involved in the region and not, as in seek to drive us away.

For the first time in decades, we can enjoy simult good relations with both China and Japan. It is di overstress the importance of this fact. Normalizat solidates a favorable balance of power in the Far I enhances the security of our friends.

Now the Chinese are turning outward and e their hand to the West. We are prepared to respon confidence that in the future their hand will rer tended than in the knowledge that without a r gesture, their hand would certainly be withdrawn.

VIEWS OF US FOREIGN POLICY
IN THE FUTURE[1]

GEORGE BUSH[2]

George Bush addressed the students at the Georgetown University School of Foreign Service on January 25, 1979. The Texan, who had served as US Ambassador to the United Nations, Director of Central Intelligence Agency, and special envoy to the People's Republic of China, spoke from a background of familiarity with many aspects of American life and foreign policy. What he said was especially pertinent in the light of the fact that he was campaigning for the Republican nomination for the presidency. It was suggested that he might have been acting as a kind of surrogate for Gerald Ford—that if the former President should announce his intentions to run again, Bush would withdraw in Ford's favor.

Arguing as a member of the Republican opposition, Bush offered a criticism of the policies of the Carter administration. Citing the ills in government and foreign policy and blaming them on the present administration, he proceeded to offer an alternate view of American policies both at home and abroad. It is evident from the speech that there is no suggestion of change in direction: but there is a plea for what Bush regards as better government, from the Republican point of view.

As we start a new year, I am struck by the volume and amplitude of anxiety felt by Americans.

In travelling about the country, I find that many are losing their confidence in the ability of our leaders—not just in politics but in education, business, and other endeavors—to cope with the problems of our time and to convey a sense of purpose and direction. Vermont Royster, a dean of American journalism, has properly said that our

---

[1] Delivered to students of School of Foreign Service, Georgetown University, Washington, D.C., January 25, 1979. Quoted by permission.
[2] For biographical note, see Appendix.

society seems to be afflicted with "free floating anxiety" about the future.

In trying to find what has happened to us, I think one answer that is quite clear is that here at home—in our domestic affairs—the organizing principles of our society have begun to crumble. During the 1930s and 1940s, a general consensus grew up in the nation that we could solve most of our social and institutional problems through the power of central government. That belief reached its zenith, perhaps, in the 1960s, but as the earthquake of Proposition 13 reminded us last summer, the 60s are now over in the United States.

We have come into a new era in which people no longer regard government as efficient, nor even benevolent. It has become too big, too powerful, too wasteful—and I am sure you could add many epithets of your own. Thus, we are in search of new organizing principles here at home.

It is worth reminding ourselves that we are by no means unique in this regard.

The bandwagon against big government is rolling through many other western nations, and where it will stop, no one really knows. This past December, one of the most thoughtful editors of the *Economist,* Norman MacRae, completed a tour of the United States, Canada, Australia, South Africa, and Britain, and in a lengthy report, he wrote that: "Across the English-speaking world, the system of Government is breaking down . . . there is probably going to be a great deal of unpleasantness as the next stage unfolds."

The challenges at home—inflation, unemployment, strengthening family life, and maintaining a sense of social cohesion—are thus much the same for all of us.

Yet, I would argue here this afternoon that in addressing these issues here at home—as we must—that we must pay no less heed to the issues that are facing us abroad, for the threat to our society from across the waters is no less important. Indeed, it appears to be mounting rapidly.

All of us have recognized for some time that the organizing principles of our domestic life were beginning to lose their staying power; but it has only been in the past few months that we have been forcefully taught that the principles of our foreign policy are also wearing thin. As our links with one nation after another are smashed to bits—Afghanistan, South Yemen, Ethiopia, and now, Iran—America can no longer turn a blind eye to what is happening in the world. It is time to sound the alarm.

After World War II, the United States developed a fairly coherent approach to world affairs, one that was supported by members of both political parties. In general, we were successful: We provided an umbrella of security for Europe and Japan to recover from their devastation; our policy encouraged the evolution of the peoples of the Third World away from colonialism and toward independence. As a result America enjoyed several years of relative prosperity and peace.

But now as we prepare for the 80s, we find that our consensus on foreign policy has been shattered. Vietnam split away millions of people, many young, some old, who concluded that America's role in the world should be curtailed. Arnold Toynbee once said that America is like a big dog in a small room: Every time it wags its tail, it knocks over a chair. But many of the anti-Vietnam protesters of the 60s thought it was much worse than that: They believed—and their beliefs were fueled by the revisionists on many of our campuses—that America is an arrogant, reactionary power that is a source of great mischief in the world. In effect, they have become the new isolationists, for they want the United States to ignore international affairs and let the world go its merry way—even if that means the destruction of free institutions and friendly countries.

On the other hand, I believe the great majority of Americans believe that America has a responsible role to play and that, if we withdraw, the world is much more likely to slide toward totalitarianism. It is among this group—and I count myself as one of them—that there is now mounting concern about the trend of recent events beyond our shores.

Our most immediate problem as a nation is that our current foreign policy seems to be one of splendid oscillation. One day, our government speaks about our responsibility as a world leader in the face of a growing Soviet menace; the next day, our President tells us that we should no longer have "an inordinate fear of communism." One day, our naval fleet is ordered from the Philippines to a position just off Iran; the next day, the signals are changed, and it is told to cut figure eights in the South China sea. One day, we inform our allies that we want their support in order to build a neutron bomb—support that Chancellor Schmidt of Germany then courageously gave us: the next day, we inexplicably announce that we do not intend to build a neutron bomb, at least for the foreseeable future. Thus, our policy has zigged and zagged from being tough one day, to soft and mushy the next.

It is this very indecisiveness, this shilly-shallying that reflects I believe both a lack of consensus within the government and within the country. Within the government itself, there appear to be major divisions between those at the highest levels, especially at the National Security Council, and those in second level position, especially in the State Department. The hawks are at NSC; the doves at State; and as they squabble, American tail feathers are being scattered around the world.

Similarly, within the country at large, there is now a lack of consensus about the nature and purpose of American power abroad. There is a distinct sense of drift. We no longer have a clear sense of what we should be doing or what kind of world we are trying to build.

When I was young, and my dad was serving in the United States Senate with Arthur Vandenberg, he always taught me it was very important that politics stop at the water's edge. And for many years it did. But with our foreign policy consensus having been hammered into oblivion on the anvil of Vietnam, times have changed. Now, as we search for a new framework for our foreign policy—just as we search for a new framework in domestic policy—I think all of us should speak our minds, recognizing that the world does not yield to simple answers and that reasonable men can disagree.

I would like to advance a few ideas that I believe are fundamental to US foreign policy in the future.

I always begin with two basic propositions.

First, I think we have to recognize that our greatest adversary in world affairs is still the Soviet Union and that the motivating force in Soviet policy is to achieve dominance in the world. It would be soothing to think that all the Soviets want to cooperate, but for reasons that strike deep into the Russian psyche, I believe that their goal is more ambitious. The evidence seems irrefutable:

Since 1962, the Soviets have poured between 14 and 18 percent of their GNP into their armed forces.

Their total spending on arms is more than 45 percent larger than US military spending, and as you know, more than half of our own defense budget goes into pensions and salaries.

As a result of their dramatic investments, Soviet ground forces now outnumber US ground forces by virtually every criterion.

The Soviets have not only built up overwhelming superiority in conventional forces but they have surpassed us in many areas of strategic armaments, including the SS–17 and the SS–19, both of which are capable of MIRVing.

Accompanying their growth in armaments has been an ambitious civil defense program.

They are also spending millions of dollars on anti-satellite technology and from public sources, we find evidence of frightening new laser research.

Finally, and equally important, we confront Soviet adventurism around the world. Their Cuban mercenaries—40,000 strong—are now planted in at least 24 different countries in Africa: their Vietnam proxies—100,000 strong—have swept aside the government in Cambodia; and the Soviets themselves are daily beaming radio broadcasts into Iran, telling the people there how perfidious the United States has been.

Personally, I do not understand how anyone could review all of the evidence without concluding that the Soviets are probing and testing our will.

And the central challenge they present is not one of overwhelming us with their nuclear weaponry—though that is always a grave possibility—but of slowly, inexorably breaking the links between the United States and its friends abroad.

That is why, in many respects, it does not necessarily serve Soviet intentions to convert Iran into a pro-Soviet state; what will serve their purposes equally well is to destroy Iran's ties to the west, turning it into a non-aligned, perhaps radicalized state with policies paralleling those of a nation like Libya. That is the true nightmare that should haunt the White House today.

The second proposition that I want to advance this afternoon is that in light of this challenge, the overreaching responsibility of the United States in world affairs is to be the leader in preserving man's hope for freedom.

The President said in his State of the Union address this week that we need a "new foundation" in foreign affairs. I completely agree. We do need a new foundation.

First, we must show more respect and understanding in the way we treat other nations that are friends and allies who share our commitments.

I deeply believe in the struggle for human rights and I believe that the United States should be the champions of that struggle; but I do not believe that we advance that goal—and certainly, we weaken our alliances and friendships—by publicly kicking around nations like Argentina and Brazil while moving closer to a repressive regime like Cuba. Similarly, I cannot understand what purpose is advanced by continually sanctioning South Africa while remaining virtually silent about the atrocities committed in Cambodia. Let us press forward for human rights, but let us do so in harmony with our other goals.

Second, I am convinced that we must put more backbone into our posture regarding the Soviet Union. We cannot confuse détente with dismissal of our world obligations: We cannot confuse accommodation with appeasement. I do not mean that we must suddenly engage in sabre rattling; negotiations must continue to be a vital part of our relationship; but I do mean that we must be willing to recognize our interests in the world and to stand firm in protecting them. As Winston Churchill said: "We cannot parley unless we arm. We cannot negotiate unless through strength."

In coming weeks, the President is likely to conclude a SALT II agreement with President Brezhnev and the nation will be pitched headlong into vigorous debate over foreign policy. With the terms of the treaty not yet available, it is premature to judge it on the merits. It is not too early, however, to express concern about the way that the President has unilaterally given up so many bargaining chips—the B-1, the neutron bomb, naval modernization, and the rest—without winning anything in return.

It is not too early to insist that in order to be acceptable, the treaty must contain adequate provisions on verification. And certainly, it is not too early to make it clear that a SALT agreement must be voted on within the context of overall Soviet behavior: The United States must not allow a nuclear weapons treaty to serve as protective cover for Soviet adventurism around the world.

Third, I believe it imperative that as a great power, the United States maintain its credibility with both friend and foe alike. Throughout the postwar period, American credibility—joined with American military strength—has been the binding force that has held the free world together. But that credibility has been badly eroded. We must reaffirm a basic principle: When the United States of America speaks, it must be believed; when it makes promises, it must keep them.

Those of you who are familiar with my record in public life know that I have long argued we should establish formal diplomatic relations with the People's Republic of China. I thus welcomed the initial effort of the current administration to move in that direction. But I was startled —and deeply dismayed—by the terms of the final agreement. The United States, incredibly enough, agreed to all three of China's basic demands—abrogation of the defense treaty, removal of our troops, and de-recognition of the Taiwan government—but abandoned the only demand that we had ever made of the Chinese:

To guarantee that the issue of Taiwan would be peacefully resolved. We gave all, and got nothing in return—and in the process, we wrecked our credibility in anxious capitals around the world, stretching from Seoul to Tel Aviv.

Unfortunately, the impression is rapidly taking hold that we have treated the Iranian question in much the same way. No one can be certain whether a government that included the Shah could be maintained, but it is abundantly clear that our on again, off again statements about him did much to hasten his departure. It is also clear, I think, that our hesitancy in responding to Soviet demands stimulated grave doubts in Iran—and frankly, in other nations such as Saudi Arabia—that we would be weak and pusilanimous in dealing with the issue.

Once again, our credibility suffered, and our influence and respect slipped several notches in other capitals. In coming years, nothing can be more important to the success of our foreign policy than to restore our credibility abroad.

A fourth conclusion that I would argue this afternoon is that in order to be a great power, we must have eyes and ears to understand what is going on around us. If the Iranian experience has taught us anything, it is surely the need for a healthy, operational intelligence community.

As one who believed that some reform was needed in our intelligence community and has appreciated many of the steps that have been taken, I would say to you that it is time to stop tearing down the CIA and to give it a new start in life.

Finally, I would urge that if we wish to be a great power in the world, then we must believe once again in our greatness as people. I was struck recently by the article written by the French playwright, Eugene Ionesco, after a stay in the United States. "Americans," he said, "want to feel guilty. They have this need to be guilty . . . (but) that masochism which keeps on haunting Americans is more dangerous than anything mankind has wreaked upon itself for centuries and centuries."

Ionesco recognizes, as should we, that this is a nation that has done as much for the cause of humanity and more for the cause of freedom than any other nation that has ever inhabited this Earth. We are a good people. We are a decent people. And, if we are vigilant, if we have the will, if we have faith in ourselves, and we rediscover our sense of purpose, then we can continue to be the single greatest force for peace that man has ever known.

That is a notable destiny, but it is a destiny that can be ours. In coming days, as a great debate unfolds about American foreign policy, let us make that once again our highest goal.

INTERNATIONAL ECONOMIC POLICY

THE YEN TO MAKE A MARK WITH THE DOLLAR [1]

FRANK CHURCH [2]

The soundness of the American dollar has been of grave concern both within the United States and abroad. Once the symbol of stability on the world market, the dollar now takes a back seat to the German mark, the Japanese yen, and the Swiss franc. Galloping inflation, a large deficit, and unfavorable trade balances have plagued the American economy and devalued the dollar abroad. Our economic policy was the subject of an address by Frank Church (Democrat, Idaho), chairman of the powerful Senate Foreign Relations Committee, to the University Forum Assembly at Brigham Young University, Provo, Utah, on December 12, 1978.

His immediate audience numbered 1,300 students and faculty and the speech was simultaneously aired on the campus FM radio station and later presented on two occasions on the university television station. Church's prominent position in the Senate ensured that the speech would receive careful attention outside of Utah and probably abroad. This cogent speech, with a title that obviously gave the speaker a good deal of fun, was "a franc look at our international economic policy" and serves as a kind of index to American thinking on monetary policy, trade restrictions, foreign aid, and even limitation of armaments.

Frank Church, tall, handsome, and direct, takes great pride in his speeches and is one of the most articulate senators. He is most effective especially in impromptu situations. Since he is chairman of the Senate Foreign Relations Committee, he is frequently called on to give his views on foreign policy matters, in person and on television. It is interesting to note that his career as chairman of the Committee has in many ways paralleled that of another Idahoan, William E. Borah, a Republican (1865–1940).

On October 25, President Carter went on television to announce that his administration was about to take a

---

[1] Delivered to a student assembly, Brigham Young University, Provo, Utah, December 12, 1978, at 10:05 A.M. Quoted by permission.

[2] For biographical note, see Appendix.

series of draconian measures designed to slow the rate of inflation at home, to bolster the dollar abroad, and to reduce our huge trade deficit. I welcomed the President's action: I felt he had no other alternative.

Perhaps the most noteworthy aspect of the President's decision is that it was neither Congressional pressure nor the direction of domestic demand that forced him to act. Rather, it was external pressure, the resounding vote of "no confidence" in the dollar in Europe and Japan, the spectre of impending worldwide financial panic which led to the sudden turnabout in administration policy. The collapsing dollar abroad finally brought home a painful truth—that America's economic position in the world has been seriously eroded over the years and that a fundamental change in our outlook was long overdue.

The dollar crisis was the culmination of a process that had been underway for at least a decade. The foreign exchange markets were merely reacting to other signs that the US economy is not faring well in its dealings with the outside world: The turn-around in our balance of trade from a healthy surplus through most of the fifties and sixties, to a chronic deficit in the seventies, which last year swelled to $27 billion; our growing dependence on foreign oil, which now accounts for half our total consumption; an earlier flight from the dollar which in 1971–72 forced two devaluations and, eventually, the demonetization of gold and a move to floating exchange rates.

The erosion of our accustomed economic predominance, I believe, is directly related to a single-minded concentration, since the Second World War, on our global power struggle with the Soviet Union. The protracted Cold War absorbed so much of our energy and attention that we failed to notice the underlying shift in the balance of economic power of the world. We failed to recognize that, while the Soviet Union may pose the only military threat to the United States, the real challenge to the American economic position came from our closest allies and trading

partners in Western Europe, the Middle East and Asia—
from Germany and Japan, from the Arab Nations, and
more recently, even from such small countries as Korea and
Taiwan. In any global contest for economic supremacy, the
Soviet Union, plagued by chronic inefficiency, low productivity, constant supply bottlenecks, and a suffocating
bureaucracy, is not even a contender. Neither is China.

In economic terms, Germany and Japan are the rising
new super powers. It is the mark and the yen, not the
ruble, that are knocking the dollar out of the box; it is
German and Japanese cars, and Korean steel and Taiwan-
ese television sets that are displacing our products in the
global marketplace; it is Saudi Arabia, and the other
OPEC States, not the Russians, which control the flow and
the price of oil, the very life-blood of our industrial economy.

If we are seeing the end of "the American Era," it is
not because we have lost the superpower race with the
Soviet Union for strategic superiority, but because we are
losing our capacity to compete with our own allies.

Since 1950, the United States has spent a stunning $2
trillion in building a colossal military machine, in arming
and equipping foreign governments, and in fighting brush-
fire wars in such distant places as Korea and Vietnam. No
other nation in the world, save the Soviet Union, has devoted such a large portion of its gross national product, or
such a major part of its government's budget, to military
expenditures. While Japan was spending an average of less
than one percent of its GNP on defense, and Germany less
than four percent since World War II, the United States
has diverted nearly ten percent to the military, or roughly
half our national budget.

This huge military build-up has, of course, been financed through taxes and government borrowing, resulting
in a massive diversion of financial resources from the private
sector to the public sector. And while defense spending has
provided thousands of jobs in private industry, it is a highly

inflationary form of job creation, in that it puts money into the hands of consumers without producing anything on which that money can be spent. None of my neighbors are out shopping for a tank, a submarine, or an intercontinental ballistic missile!

The emphasis on military spending has also resulted in much of our national research being directed to this purpose. While only about five percent of the Japanese R & D budget is earmarked for defense, and 25 percent of Germany's, over 70 percent of our government's R & D budget goes for military or aerospace projects. And since most of these projects are contracted out to private firms, much of the capacity for technical innovation that exists in our private sector is being consumed by the search for ever-more sophisticated armaments, rather than for developing consumer products which can compete successfully in the global marketplace. It is no coincidence that weapons have become our leading export, followed by raw food products like soybeans and wheat. . . . A rather perplexing mix for a nation that prides itself in being the world's foremost technological power!

Because our struggle with the USSR is also ideological, we have believed it necessary to spend additional billions on foreign aid, presumably to keep other governments pro-American. Since 1946, we have spent some $200 billion for such assistance, spread among 145 foreign governments. Some of this money has been put to good use, rebuilding Western Europe and bringing a measure of humanitarian relief to certain impoverished lands. But as often, this money has gone, not for needed development, but in futile efforts to prop up anti-communist governments which were too repressive or too corrupt to survive on their own.

Finally, it was to bind the ancient kingdoms of the oil rich Persian Gulf firmly to the West that the United States, in the early 1950s, helped to tie up virtually all of the oil production concessions in that area for a handful of American and British oil companies. We, in effect, condoned the establishment of a giant oil company cartel, which, in turn, served as the doormat for the emergence of OPEC, the cartel of foreign oil-producing governments which, in 1973, quadrupled the price of oil. That decision shook the economic foundations of the Western World. It set off an inflation that still rages. It threw the world credit system precariously out of balance, and heaped debt on the poorest countries. The wound it inflicted upon the Western industrial nations was far more serious than any we have suffered from the Communists. Yet, in our preoccupation with the Cold War, we did not closely monitor the vital signs of our domestic economy nor heed the clear indications that we were heading for trouble.

The strongest danger signal was the relative decline in per-man-hour productivity in the United States as compared with other industrial countries. While per-man-hour output, since 1964, has been increasing at an average annual rate of 9.3 percent in Japan, 6.4 percent in France, and 6.3 percent in Germany, US output has grown by only 1.7 percent. Even the British performance is better, at 2.8 percent. What's more, the US trend is downward. Overall, our annual productivity gains since 1970 have been only about half the rate of the previous two decades.

Of course, one must keep in mind that Germany and Japan began the post war period at a far lower original level of productivity than the United States. Nevertheless, their rapid improvement is evidence of an economic vitality that is sadly lacking in our own country. Compared to our main economic competitors, we seem to be standing practically still, and the great competitive advantage with which we started the second half of this century is being frittered away.

There can be no quick fixes, no instant solutions to our present predicament. The answer can only be found at home, in a resurgent domestic economy—not in any intertional trade system rigged in our favor.

Past efforts in this direction have, predictably, failed. For example, under intense pressure from the US Government, Japan volunteered last year to reduce its exports of certain products to the United States, including autos, steel, and television sets. True to their promises, the Japanese cut back their shipments of color TV's to us by 530,000 sets in the first four months of 1978, down 25 percent from the year before. But who made up the difference in the market? Not American producers. No. It was Taiwan and Korea that took up the slack. In the same period, Taiwan's television exports to the United States increased by 326 percent, and Korea's by 155 percent. Mexico's sales also rose, by 22 percent. Thus, the net impact of Japan's restraint on US trading accounts was nil.

The real answer to our economic woes lies in a rejuvenation of the American economy. A resurgent domestic economy is essential to maintaining our competitive standing; indeed, it is the key to America's overall position of power and influence in the world. If we can solve our domestic problems, the external economic difficulties we face, such as our huge trade deficit and the weakness of the dollar, will soon take care of themselves.

Fortunately, the necessity for this kind of national undertaking is now widely recognized and the process has already begun.

The first step taken by Congress this year was to provide greater incentive for private savings and investment. For example, the maximum tax rate on capital gains was reduced from 49 percent to 28 percent, which should provide a needed stimulus to the stock market. The tax bill also reduced the corporate income tax rate from 48 percent to 46 percent. Moreover, smaller companies, with a taxable income of less than $100,000, will be subject to a much more favorable, graduated rate, starting at 17 percent. And continuation of the 10 percent investment tax credit should encourage companies to plow their added disposable income into new plants and equipment.

Of equal importance is President Carter's strong commitment to the fight against inflation. He recognizes that deficit spending is one of the causes of inflation, and has therefore recommended substantial budget cuts in virtually all government programs. If the President and the Congress continue to work together, there is hope of balancing the budget by 1981.

Balancing the budget will have the added benefit of freeing up more investment capital for private industry. Corporations borrowing in the private capital markets now must compete for credit directly with the government. This year, the federal government's demand for credit will total some $90 billion, almost equal to the $100 billion all private corporations are expected to borrow. Elimination of the deficit will eliminate the government's need to borrow, and thus both increase the amount of money available to the private sector and reduce the cost of credit.

Another important step to stem the tide of inflation was taken earlier this year when the President moved to deregulate the airline industry. That C.A.B. action has now been followed by dismantling certain competitive restraints in the trucking industry. I hope more will follow. Deregulation—abolishing the myriad of government regulations and subsidies that act as a damper on competition—may be one of the most effective anti-inflation tools we possess.

But government is not the only engine of inflation: big business and big labor must share the blame. Neither labor nor management has yet shown any willingness to exercise self-restraint. Being fully convinced that prices will continue to rise, unions press their demands for higher wages and fringe benefits. Management, in turn, has little incentive to resist these demands or to absorb the cost by reducing profits: higher wages are simply passed on to the consumer in the form of higher prices. Hopefully, both sides will come to see that their mutual interest will be better served by voluntary compliance with the guidelines recently proposed by the President.

But if a healthy and vigorous domestic economy is the key to our international standing, then our foreign policy should be refashioned to promote this goal. Much greater emphasis must be given to economic considerations—subject only to the caveat that this be done without sacrificing our national security.

I believe a number of things can be done to assist the process of economic rejuvenation without damaging our national security. One, is the completion of an acceptable strategic arms limitation agreement with the Soviet Union.

Without such an agreement, our strategic defense costs will have to rise dramatically in the next decade if we are to keep up with the arms build-up projected for the Soviet Union. The Senate Budget Committee staff has estimated that over the next 15 years, the incremental cost to the United States of a resumed all-out nuclear arms race envisioned in the absence of a SALT agreement, would amount to an extra $100 billion.

The irony is that we would be spending these billions on weapons no national leader would ever use, for their use would surely trigger the annihilation of our own people. A mutual and balanced reduction of these nuclear arsenals—a de-escalation of the strategic arms race—would actually lower the level of danger to us and to the Russians while, at the same time, provide great financial savings.

Secondly, our foreign aid program should be subjected to much more careful scrutiny. There is nothing sacrosanct about foreign aid, and I see no reason to exempt it from across-the-board cuts that will apply to the rest of the budget.

Furthermore, the time has come to stop subsidizing private investment abroad. While such investment no doubt contributes to economic development in poor countries, I see no reason why our own government should continue to prod our own corporations to invest abroad, when the money is so badly needed here at home.

The special tax incentives for US corporations to invest

abroad—incentives that compete directly with, and to some degree, negate domestic investment—should be eliminated. Chief among these is the provision that allows American-owned corporations to defer paying taxes on earnings from overseas operations indefinitely, unless or until such earnings are actually repatriated. This provision, naturally, encourages companies to reinvest their foreign earnings abroad, thus avoiding ever having to pay the American income tax. I will try again next year to strike this deferral from our statute books.

Likewise, I intend to continue my efforts to terminate a federal agency known as the Overseas Private Investment Corporation—which provides political risk insurance for our multinational corporations which invest in foreign lands. The higher return which foreign investments typically yield should be more than enough to cover any political risk involved. And, if not, let the companies pay for private insurance coverage and keep the US Government out of it.

Finally, we must reassess our international energy policy. "Special relationships" with a few oil-rich countries, which is the essence of our present oil policy, are no substitute in the long run for a diversity of supply. And they most certainly are no guarantee against higher prices, nor even against economic blackmail, as we learned in 1973. Quite the contrary.

The rebellion in Iran, which has seriously interrupted oil production there, should teach us the extreme folly of becoming too reliant on any one ruler or small group of rulers—no matter how pro-American—for the supply of a vital commodity such as oil. No matter how much trade and aid, no matter how many weapons we provide them, we cannot eliminate the fundamental fragility of these feudal regimes trying to govern societies which are undergoing a rapid and wrenching modernization.

It now appears that we have a new oil and gas bonanza just south of the border in Mexico. It is in our interest to promote the rapid development of those resources, not only to diversify our sources of imported energy, but also to reduce the economic, social, and political pressures which the proximity of that impoverished land exerts on our own country. The future of Mexico should be of just as much concern to the US—if not more—than the future of the Shah or the Sheiks of the Arabian Peninsula.

In sum, I believe that we must pursue a foreign policy that serves our national economic interest: a policy that recognizes that our long-term strength, including our national security, depends even more upon the vitality of the American economy than upon the size of our armed forces. A ship of state is not necessarily more seaworthy because she carries lots of cannon—indeed, without a sturdy hull, she is more likely to capsize and sink. Perhaps it is time to throw overboard some of the ballast we have carried with us in the Cold War, to acknowledge that we do have interests in the international arena that go beyond the parameters of the East-West struggle. And these interests, and our place in the world, cannot be protected without a change in course.

I will do what I can as the next Chairman of the Foreign Relations Committee to shift the focus of our foreign policy to the issues I have discussed today, and to see to it that economic matters are given the emphasis they deserve. Because I have a Yen to make a Mark for the Dollar.

ECONOMIC INTERDEPENDENCE: THE WORLD AT A CROSSROADS[1]

Adlai Stevenson III[2]

On December 13, 1978 Adlai Stevenson III, Senator from Illinois (Democrat), addressed the Annual Conference of the Institute for Socioeconomic Studies, held at the Park Lane Hotel in New York City. The conferees were 100 leaders from public affairs, business and finance, and the professions. The Institute is "a non-profit foundation with broad research interests relating to the quality of life, economic developments, social motivation, poverty, urban regeneration, and problems of the elderly."

Prior to Senator Stevenson's speech, Dr. Leonard M. Greene, President of the Institute, had presented its National Service Award to Senator Daniel Patrick Moynihan (New York, Democrat) and to Vernon E. Jordan, Jr., President of Urban League. Since Senator Moynihan could not be present because he was attending the funeral of Golda Meir, he was represented by his wife Elizabeth Brennan Moynihan. In his speech Senator Stevenson makes reference to the two recipients.

The address was of the formal lecture type, and its careful preparation suggested that the Senator recognized that his audience understood the complexities of international trade and foreign relations. Indeed, Senator Stevenson had been invited because of his expertise in these fields. In his introduction of the Senator, Dr. Leonard M. Greene, President of the Institute, said, "As Chairman of the Senate Subcommittee on International Finance, he brings to the Annual Conference a wealth of experience to help us find answers to these difficult problems."

What is reproduced here appears to be a verbatim transcript of the Stevenson speech. Noticeable in this version are impromptu insertions that the speaker included during delivery (based upon a comparison of press release and printed proceedings). It is

---

[1] Delivered at the Annual Conference of the Institute for Socioeconomic Studies, Park Lane Hotel, New York City, 8 P.M., December 13, 1978. Published in the *Journal of the Socioeconomic Studies,* IV (Spring 1979), 51–83. Quoted by permission.

[2] For biographical note, see Appendix.

much less formal than the typescript provided by the Senator's office.

The speech is comparatively simple in its structure. After taking note of the awards presented and some good natured chiding of his fellow senator, Stevenson launched into his carefully conceived constructive argument, following a problem-solution organization.

This dinner is a monument to the ingenuity and spirit of Dr. Greene and I am honored and very grateful for the opportunity to be a part of it.

Vernon Jordan is a champion of social justice in America, and richly deserving of the *Award* which he has been given tonight.

Elizabeth Moynihan: if I were in my own state, my constituents would say that we have all got the better half. But much as it is a pleasure to be here with all of you and Elizabeth, I am disappointed that my good friend and colleague, Pat Moynihan, is not with us. I don't have a chance to speak very often while he listens.

I don't want to suggest that there were no other reasons for coming here tonight, but I had thought that this might be a chance to compel some attention from a good friend, my colleague from New York.

He is a friend and he, too, is richly deserving of the Institute's *Award*.

I am told that if I proceed to do my duty, which is to speak to you, and if you do your duty, which is to listen to me, that there may be an opportunity afterwards, assuming some survivors, for a chance to exchange ideas and for you to make suggestions and ask questions of me. And that being the case, I would like to get on with my duty, which, as Dr. Greene indicated, reflects some responsibilities of mine, including those of the Chairman of the Subcommittee on International Finance of the Senate, which has jurisdiction over trade, money exports—the position of the United States in the new global economy of the world.

In the 1970s, food prices rose with wheat sales to the Soviet Union; energy price increases rippled out to inflate the price of every commodity and service in every stage in their production and distribution. The monetary systems forged at Bretton Woods collapsed. International liquidity increased to five times the annual rate of the 1960s, and the nation suffered double digit inflation, recession, and high unemployment. This phenomenon of simultaneous inflation and economic stagnation is significant in itself—but more so as a symptom of change to which other nations, more disciplined and pragmatic, are adjusting more readily than we. This is a highly competitive, interdependent world for which the appropriate policies and institutions are not devised.

Bismarck, the Iron Chancellor, once remarked somewhat enviously, "God holds his hand particularly over fools, drunkards and the United States of America."

After having prepared these remarks, I came across another quote which I will share with you. This one is from Lord Brice. He said: "Safe from attack, even from menace, she hears from afar the warring cries of European nations and faiths, for the present at least. It may not always be so. America sails upon the summer sea."

My suggestion, my message tonight is that it is no longer so. The development of the United States was fueled by something more than the genius proclaimed by Fourth of July orators. It was fueled by labor from Africa and Europe, by abundant raw materials, including oil and seemingly endless frontiers. For a time recently, the United States controlled the world's capital. Its technology was pre-eminent. But all that is abruptly changed.

Now economic interdependence is more than a cliche. We are left to compete in a highly competitive world with many of our natural advantages, if not God's hand, withdrawn. Nations are each dependent on others for food and energy, for markets and supplies, for technology and capital —and this nation is no exception. The United States must scramble for its share of the world's resources and markets. And it is left to do so with a government intimidated by new ideas and the public reaction to the grossness of recent years. The dollar has declined like a barometer of world confidence in our ability to discipline ourselves and compete. A few weeks ago, the world was close to the brink of financial panic only to be pulled back by emergency measures to rescue the dollar. But next year the American balance of payments deficit may be somewhat reduced by gold sales and lower growth rates in the United States than in some nations abroad. But our measures, I think, are only reflexive. They deal with symptoms and rarely address the phenomena which gave rise to the necessity for them. High interest rates and indiscriminate budget cuts will retard investment at cost to the production of goods and services and cause stagnation which will be followed by more budget deficits and declining growth rates the world over.

Without some attention to increased productivity and the institutions of world commerce, these measures offer a high risk of inflation, recession, and political instability. The economic and political imponderables of an undisciplined world increase the risk of failure for policies modeled on abstractions from the eighteenth century.

It seems to me that the contest of ideas in America has crossed party lines. Some—under both parties—would return to the stand pat system of the 1950s, others would enlarge upon the welfare statism of the 60s, some would go back to the Cold War, while others would turn to a benign form of global neglect. (And that, Elizabeth, was written with a view to your husband!—not that he is in favor of *that* kind of neglect.) Tragically, these contending sides ignore the preconditions of social progress and national security in an age of global interdependence.

In the late 1940s, the United States acted with vision, as it had not 20 years earlier. It led the rebirth of the Free World. More than any other nation, the United States created the post-war institutions of trade and finance which brought the world a measure of sustained peace and prosperity.

Now the world is again at a crossroads. World population may increase by 50 percent before the end of the century. Already much of mankind is living close to the margins of existence, as sources of food and fuel are depleted or priced out of reach. Nations, dependent on each other, are moved by economic expediencies and animosities spawned by history and ideology to seek independence. The invisible hand of Adam Smith has become the visible hand of government subsidizing exports and restricting imports. Cartels in the United States and other interests stand the law of supply and demand on its head. Much of the world acknowledges no such thing as a free market. And where the price mechanism is relied upon to allocate goods and resources, other factors are at work. The price mechanism does not automatically redress a balance of payments deficit, as was confidently predicted by the theoreticians when the dollar was unlinked from gold.

Western Europe had a two percent growth last year. Growth rates will not be high enough to prevent unemployment from rising in nearly every market country next year. Inflation rages and world trade is stagnant. International debt has quintupled since the oil price hikes in 1973. The credit requirements of nations and industries exceed the resources of official and commercial credit facilities. Consumer debt at home has reached $300 billion, much of it incurred in anticipation of inflation. Investment in productive enterprise and innovation is flagging the world over. And payments are aggravated by the continued failure of nations to conserve energy and expand energy supplies. This is not a condition which will be improved by 12 percent interest rates and indiscriminate budget cuts for everything except defense.

In the 20s, the United States failed to offer the world economic leadership and it invited world depression. Depression, with all of the inadequacies of the first war's settlement, led to the next war.

The United States could again acquiesce in the economic—political turbulence of which Iran is a portent. Or our nation could act to restore its authority in the world by renewing the institutions of world finance and trade, and by broadening the framework for global cooperation.

Reform of the international monetary system began with American leadership at Bretton Woods. Now, international exchange uncertainties are depressing world commerce and facilities for the financing of payments are limited. American leadership could develop a universal monetary system which included the OPEC surplus countries and the non-market countries. It would bring down artificial barriers between East and West, bring in OPEC surpluses and move the world toward freely convertible currencies and a universal medium of exchange.

An America committed to cooperation instead of confrontation, to involvement instead of isolation, should mount an effort to ensure capital for the production of raw materials, manufactures, and other goods and services in the world. The World Bank's program to stimulate energy, research and production in the developing countries is a step in the right direction. The United States could join with other nations in new institutional means of investing capital and technology worldwide in the production of energy. Unfortunately, our nation is, instead, still preoccupied with an illusory notion of energy independence.

Sweden and Canada have established foundations which facilitate the application of technology to the development of the least developed nations. The United States could join that effort. It could still lead it.

We might with more vision implement the demand management policies of the past with global supply management policies for the future and come to grips with the dominant cause of inflation—and the dangers of depression. Contrary to the logic of demand management, inflation now accompanies unemployment. With some imagination, growth might be associated with stable prices. Investment in the production of essential goods and services is an altogether more promising means of controlling inflation than decreasing demand for them. It also is the key to practical stability and the nation's security. Iran should remind us that the instability of a critical regime is rooted more so in the indigenous sources of discontent than the external sources of subversion which exploit them.

In 1951, Japan had two percent of international exports. Today it has eight percent. In the same period the US share of exports declined from 20 percent to 12 percent. And now a new wave of competition looms from LDCs [less developed countries] and non-market countries combining high technology, low labor costs and priorities that rank social welfare benefits and environmental protection behind development. China is moving to harness its natural resources, and 800 million disciplined, industrious people through its economic development. The China card players, if any there are, might do well to ponder the possibilities of that armed, militant, industrious, resourceful nation come 20 years from now.

But instead of leading the foreign competition, we seek to protect ourselves from it.

This year the Congress passed legislation to undermine the trade negotiations by taking textiles out of them. Congress is pressured to follow the British course of protecting and subsidizing failing industries at the expense of all industry, dragging the country down instead of moving ahead, as do the Japanese, to develop new markets, new products, and new industries.

A 40 percent tariff cut would generate about $125 billion in additional trade for the industrial countries alone. The United States would net a gain of about 120,000 jobs. Reductions in barriers to agricultural trade and a reduction of non-tariff barriers would add hundreds of billions of dollars more in economic benefits for all participating countries. But we may go the other way. And even if the Tokyo Round [package of international trade agreements] is completed and approved, it will be time for another. This battle of reciprocal advantage versus reciprocal disadvantage never ends.

A new America would seek to bring more nations and more items of commerce into the negotiations and develop the institutional means of disciplining world trade that would review complaints about unfair trade practices, disclose such practices and develop means of enforcing codes of fair trade.

Instead of protecting ourselves from foreign competition we could set out to meet it and benefit from it. Competition rewards efficiency and stimulates innovation. In this age of administered prices, foreign competition is sometimes the only effective competition. It is deflationary.

Conventional wisdom attributes the trade deficit to oil imports. Obviously an oil bill of $40 billion is a major cause of that deficit. But other nations more dependent on foreign sources of raw materials, including fuels, run trade surpluses. And if you eliminate the US-OPEC trade deficit, you find that the US trade is still in deficit. Dependence on more expensive foreign oil will grow. And so will foreign competition.

In 1976, the United States had a $12 billion trade surplus in manufactured goods—I'm particularly thinking of IBM here. Now, our country is running a trade deficit in manufactured goods. The United States could compete by improving its productivity and its capacity for industrial innovation, developing and producing competitive products and marketing them aggressively.

The opportunities are large, but the vision and, at least from where I sit in the Senate—if not Pat Moynihan—the will is very short. (I think he would agree!)

Labor seeks protection. Business seeks more export subsidies. The administration seeks to take them away. Only the farmers seem aware of the global dimension of the market. And they would price themselves out of it!

The United States is asleep. It would be a more credible negotiator in trade talks if it demonstrated that it was not only prepared to protect its own markets against unfair trade, but also prepared to penetrate foreign markets with whatever it takes.

Exports are the province of IBM and Caterpillar—from Illinois!—and are essentially the preserve of the largest American corporations. Small corporations are left out except as suppliers to the large. Already there is scarcely an American product that is unique in the world. The quality of American products is sometimes inferior. Our global marketing is often weak especially when compared to Japanese trading companies. American productivity is weighted down by unnecessary transactional and societal costs. Our rate of productivity, again, is lower than in any industrial country except for Britain. Between 1975 and 1978, productivity increased by over 20 percent in Japan; by two percent a year in the United States. Foreign governments go all out to pay the oil bill and beat us with barriers to our imports, subsidies for their exports and support for the development of their export industry.

In the United States, the effort to develop a comprehensive export policy to enhance our competitiveness in the highly competitive new world, is only now beginning. And this effort is hindered by the consuming notion that every affliction of mankind can be cured by another law or by the withholding of American patrimony from errant nations.

The Congress has great difficulty resisting the temptation to legislate the conduct of foreign policy for which it is neither competent nor intended by the Constitution. Its efforts to condition US participation in world commerce upon the extraterritorial reach of our laws and our social priorities—and the opposition of business to them—imply that the economic, political, and moral purposes of the United States do not coincide.

A more hopeful and ultimately more humane basis from which to proceed is to recognize that such interests converge. The anti-boycott law effectively reconciled the protection of American sovereignty with a recognition of its economic interest in the Middle East. Instead of conditioning trade with non-market countries on their immigration policies, Most Favored Nation status and credits could be subjected to periodic review in Congress and the Executive branch, thereby implying that the continued availability of both would depend on Soviet conduct in terms of a broader range of US interests. Both political and economic objectives could be served by a process which normalized the commercial relationship while making it clear that the extent of that relationship depends upon a continuing accommodation of political interests across the whole spectrum.

It is imprudent for one side—be it business, be it labor, be it the environmentalists or prominent, religiously affiliated organizations—to go all out to beat the other. One side, and therefore at least one interest of the United States, is likely to be defeated unnecessarily. A more accommodating and pragmatic outlook in this world is, it seems to me, necessary if we are to stop inflicting damage to our inseparable economic and strategic interests—if we are, in short, to stop shooting ourselves in the foot.

The competitiveness of the United States in this competitive world will require a good deal more than Ex-Im Bank and Commodity Credit Corporation credits and the tax incentives which are most commonly mentioned.

In the name of competition, anti-trust laws sometimes prevent effective competition by the United States in the global marketplace. We ought to permit trading companies which could represent small as well as large American businesses throughout the world, absorbing exchange rate fluctuations on a day-to-day basis and meeting foreign competition everywhere. The commercial banks could be involved in a major effort to educate businesses, especially the small businesses, to the opportunities and methods of exporting, servicing and facilitating their export transactions. The United States could package large export transactions including everything from nuclear power plants to Caterpillar tractors from Peoria.

Trading companies with government cooperation facilitated by a new Department of Trade could help put such a package together. And such a Department, consolidating international trade and investment responsibilities, would help centralize accountability and elevate the job to one of prominence and authority in the United States, as in other nations.

Agricultural policy should be reviewed—I can say this a little bit more confidently in New York than I can back home in the largest agricultural producing state in the United States. Instead of paying farmers to decrease the production of food, while supporting food prices at artificial levels, farmers could be encouraged to produce food at prices determined by the marketplace. As it is, we react to last year's surplus, instead of tomorrow's hunger, and price food out of world markets. Farmers could be supported with cash payments to whatever extent is necessary while food prices are allowed to find a market level with deflationary consequences at home, as well as enlarged market opportunities for meat and grain producers abroad.

I have been in Poland recently. Our Illinois soy beans go to Poland and then we buy back the hams from Poland. We might, with a more sensible policy, sell them the hams!

If barriers to exports—meat exports—come down in Japan, who will move in? As things now stand, I suspect it will be the Australians and the New Zealanders.

It would be a far more efficient means of distributing food throughout the world to do it with meat instead of food grains with which to produce the meat. We have our policies!—and they have priced our meat producers out of this global market. Moreover, to a large extent, we have also priced our grain producers out of the market.

Technology is the basis of our ability to compete. The most technology-oriented industries, aerospace for example, are the most competitive and export-oriented. Instead of subsidizing non-competitive industries along the British line, the government might with more wisdom assist in the development of new industries, new products and new manufacturing processes as do more aggressive nations. US investment in R & D is declining in relation to the other countries, and US industry has been shifting investment from innovation to product improvement with an eye to next month's profit and loss statement instead of the next decade's. In the 1960s, hundreds of small technology-oriented companies were formed each year in the United States. By 1977, the number had reached zero. To retain our technological pre-eminence requires tax incentives for capital formation and R & D and institutes to combine the research efforts of government, academia and industry in order to develop means of applying technology to the commercialization of technology. The development of industrial processes must be included, no less than manufactures themselves. Other countries are generating such means of creating new products *and* manufacturing processes—but our nation is not.

The adversarial relationship between industry, labor and government could be put behind us, as in other countries. While the Japanese government—now this is relevant to IBM!—is combining and subsidizing its electronic data processing industry, the United States is trying to break it up—and IBM is not the only example. And next year IBM, I am told, will encounter the fourth generation of Japanese computers—am I right?—and that's about as high as technology gets, I think.

And with that, there really won't be any more unique American products in the world, though there could be. It is time the United States awoke and gave itself and the world the leadership of which it is capable. We have wandered, like Gulliver, into the land of Lilliputia, tied down by strands of minutia, reorganization plans, zero-based budgets—not to mention the Proposition 13's which are only now coming on stream. The growth industries of

America have become the law, accounting firms, the gambling businesses, and government itself—and I say that with great respect for us lawyers.

We would with more imagination restore the old entrepreneurial spirit—now under assault from impersonalized forces of government, labor, and business—and the animating Jeffersonian ideas of excellence and individual freedom now threatened by an egalitarian ethic. Sadly, we seek to redistribute profit at some risk of no longer making it.

The capacity of democratic governments everywhere to act decisively is in doubt. The governments of most industrialized nations are weak. In the third world they are often unstable and susceptible to forces of internal dissatisfaction and sometimes external subversion. And we are preoccupied with unproductive and unusable weapons systems and economic and political orthodoxies better suited to the past than the turbulent and interdependent world in which we live.

America could move to meet the competition of the world. It could develop new marketing systems. It could increase the production of food. It could adapt its antitrust laws to a new global market. It could recommit itself to basic science and technological innovation; the new frontiers in space could be pushed back with the American space shuttle and that benign environment could be utilized routinely for the benefit of mankind, with the strategic arms race barred from entering it. America can recognize that it is more promising for mankind to increase the production of essential commodities and services than to decrease the demand.

It could move as it did in the late 40s to build world institutions of trade, money, development. It could recognize that common action is the only way to deal with common problems. There is no limit to what the world could do with America's ingenuity, America's entrepreneurship, and not a new but an old order of American statesmanship.

PRESS FREEDOMS

WHAT THE PEOPLE GRANT, THEY CAN TAKE AWAY [1]

Vermont C. Royster [2]

At a time when it could be argued that they should be grateful for the investigative activities of the press, many citizens have become suspicious that reporters are partisan in their coverage of public affairs. Past administrations have complained of harassment by the media. Indeed, televised presidential press conferences suggest that an adversary relation exists between the President and reporters and sometimes a questioner seems more eager to put the Chief Executive on the spot than to seek clarification of an important issue. Now warnings are coming from leaders of the mass media that the attitudes of the press—or at least of some of its members—is creating public ill will that could lead to curtailment of a free press. In the light of this atmosphere, Vermont Royster's remarks are timely.

On December 5, 1978, Royster became the sixth recipient of the Fourth Estate Award of the National Press Club of Washington, D.C. At the awards dinner held in the Grand Ballroom of the National Press Club were about 300 persons representing "a wider spectrum of publishing and broadcasting and related fields."

This award recognized "excellence and outstanding contributions during the entire working career of the recipient." Others to receive the plaudit earlier have included Walter Cronkite of CBS News (1973), James Reston of the New York *Times* (1974), Richard Strout of the *Christian Science Monitor* (1975), John S. Knight of the Knight-Ridder Newspapers (1976), and Herbert Block of the Washington *Post* (1977).

In response to this recognition Mr. Royster, who formerly was on the staff of the *Wall Street Journal* and presently is a professor of Journalism at the University of North Carolina, reminisced about his experiences as a journalist and discussed the role the press should play in contemporary society. He warned his colleagues against abusing the freedoms that have been granted the press under the First Amendment.

---

[1] Delivered at Awards Luncheon, National Press Club, Washington, D.C., December 5, 1978. Quoted by permission.

[2] For biographical note, see Appendix.

It's hardly necessary for me to say how pleased and honored I am to be here this evening, in this Club, before this audience.

Of all the moments of recognition that may come to a man in his lifetime, none is more deeply felt than that which comes from his peers.

That is especially true for me tonight because of those who have previously received this award. You make me a member of a very distinguished company. For that I am most grateful.

But must confess I am also embarrassed. When I received the invitation to this dinner I did not realize there was a conspiracy afoot—among old friends, my wife, and present colleagues—to turn the evening into a "this is your life" affair, one that would make it for me an evening overflowing with nostalgia.

I didn't realize I would have to sit here and listen to people, one of them from my distant past, talk about me. That is embarrassing—even though I accept all words of praise as being richly deserved!

However I am chastened by recalling something Arthur Krock said to me some years ago. He remarked that no newspaperman was ever treated as a "distinguished journalist" until he was either dead or decrepit. And since I am, happily, still alive I am left with that other alternative.

In any event, I have to admit having arrived at an age where one's thoughts about the present are entangled with memories of the past. And it's always dangerous to stir an old man's memories. He is much too apt to bore you with tales of how it was in the "olden days," and to fill the air with lamentations about their passing.

For example, I remember this Club when the room we are now in was little more than an unfinished barn and the Club itself was on the ragged edge of survival.

I remember when the Washington press corps, in total, numbered only a few hundred and you could know almost all of them by sight. There was no radio and television press gallery, not even a gallery to accommodate the periodical press. Today I am stunned by the number of pages it takes in the Congressional Directory to list the accredited press in all its forms; I refuse to use that word "media."

That was not all that was different. I well remember my first Presidential press conference. For the record, the date was Friday, May 15, 1936—more than 40 years ago—and Franklin D. Roosevelt was holding his 295th press conference since becoming President.

I presented my shiny new press credentials to the guard at the Pennsylvania Avenue gate, walked up the winding driveway and entered the West Wing of the White House.

To the left of this room was a modest office for Steve Early, the President's press secretary. Beyond and out of sight were offices for Marvin McIntyre, the President's only other regular aide, and for Missy Le Hand, his private secretary. There were two others, designated as executive clerks. And that was all. The entire White House staff.

The press conference itself was held in the Oval Office. There was only a handful of reporters gathered, lined up behind Fred Storm of the UP, a huge, hulking man who had the privilege of being the first to enter. Occasionally he rapped on the door leading from the reception hall and then laughed loudly at his feigned impatience.

Someone in the crowd joked, "His Excellency is keeping the press waiting!" But it was all good natured. At 22 years old I was awed and envious of the camaraderie.

Actually I had no business being there; the White House was far above my assignment. So I stood in the back trying to hide from Claude Mahoney, the *Wall Street Journal*'s White House correspondent, and Alfred F. ("Mike") Flynn, its senior Washington reporter. I was afraid they would think me too forward for a neophyte.

When the door opened, we gathered around the President's desk, no more than 20 of us. It wasn't a historic press conference. About all I remember of it was some casual talk about how the President was going down the Potomac on the presidential yacht and would be back Sunday night. There were some desultory questions but I find no notes among my memorabilia. I remember only being overcome at being a few feet away from the President, at being one of the little band entitled to this privilege.

Press conferences of Cabinet officials were equally informal. The Agriculture Department was my first beat and usually only four or five of us would meet with Henry Wallace in his office. No microphones. No snaking cables for lights and television cameras. It was no different with Henry Morgenthau, or Harold Ickes, or Cordell Hull.

In those days all the major government departments were within easy walking distance—Agriculture, Treasury, State, the White House, even War and Navy—and since the *Journal* office was then equally informally organized I would often wander to other press conferences, not because journalistic duty demanded it but simply because it was fun and helped give a feel for the whole of government.

Incidentally, I would drift to the State Department for another reason. My wife, Frances, worked there as a secretary when we were first married—and made more money than I did as a Washington correspondent!

The working rules for press conferences were, by and large, those applied by the President. In general we could paraphrase what he said but could use no direct quotes without express permission. He could also give us information "for background only" which we could make use of but not attribute to him. And he kept the privilege of going "off the record" entirely when he chose.

I do not need to tell you how different it is today. That old State Department building has become the Executive Office Building and it houses more staff aides to the President than, in those olden days, there were members of the press corps.

Presidential press conferences are now TV events. The last one I attended was in the time of Gerald Ford, and I swore I would never attend another. Unless you want to get your face on television there's not much point to it.

Press conferences of cabinet officers and other high government officials are also now staged with almost equal panoply.

Though I am reluctant to admit it, there are some gains in the way the new technology has altered the manner of doing things. The ordinary citizen today does get a chance to see the President in action and doubtless to form impressions not just by what the President says but by his style. His grace under pressure, or his lack of it, is not wholly irrelevant to his performance as our national leader.

The same is true of course of others in the public arena, a Secretary of State speaking on some matter of foreign policy, an economic adviser testifying before a Congressional committee. Even a 10-second snippet on the evening news tells us something about the person, and that too is not irrelevant to his public performance.

But I am not persuaded that the technological changes are all for the better. President Roosevelt could, and often did, just think out loud without fear that every word was put indelibly on the record. He could share with the reporters around his desk some information that would help them to do their jobs better, help them understand what was involved in some public question. He could, and sometimes did, misstate himself at first expression, as everyone may do in casual conversation, and then on second thought rephrase his remarks.

The modern President has no such latitude. He must live in constant fear of the slip-of-the-tongue. A misstated name from a lapse of memory can be an embarrassment. Awkward phraseology on some matter of public import is beyond recall or correction; it is flashed around the world irretrievably.

One consequence of this, it seems to me, is that Presidents today try to say no more at a press conference than what might be put as well in a carefully drafted statement. The loss here is both to the President and to the press.

The President has lost an opportunity to be frank and open. The press has lost an opportunity to share his thought processes which, without being the stuff of tomorrow's headlines, nonetheless could help them on their own to do a better job of informing their readers and listeners.

I might add, by the way, that the President has also lost the opportunity to deal bluntly with the stupid question, not unknown at a presidential press conference. Anyway, I cannot imagine President Carter telling a reporter on television that he had asked a silly question and to go stand in the dunce corner, something President Roosevelt didn't hesitate to do.

So much for the changes wrought by technology, with their advantages and disadvantages. There are also, I think, more subtle differences in the relationship between the press and government as it was and as it is. The surface differences capsule more profound changes—in our government, in our craft, and not least in the role this journalistic craft plays in the society in which we live.

I have heard it said that the old relationship between the Washington press corps and the government was too "cozy." The implication is that we were "taken in" by the informality of, let us say, Mr. Roosevelt's press conferences or the more casual relationship between the few regulars around a cabinet officer. That we were too flattered at being admitted as at least semi-insiders, too easily accepting the off-the-record conversation. That all this somehow intimidated us from doing our job.

I don't believe it. The competitive instinct among reporters then was no less than now. On my first beat, Agriculture, Felix Belair of the New York *Times* knocked naivety out of me in a hurry and he never seemed to be intimidated by Henry Wallace. I never noticed Eddie Folliard of the *Post,* Turner Catledge of the *Times* or Harrison Salisbury of the UP passing up a good story out of deference to authority.

Investigative reporting isn't new, either. It was the press that exposed the Teapot Dome scandal. In my time—for one example—Tom Stokes of Scripps-Howard won his Pulitzer for exposing graft and corruption in the WPA. The defeat of FDR's court-packing scheme was due to the spotlight the press kept on it.

But there was one thing about the press then, I think, which was different from today. We did not think of ourselves and the government as enemies.

We were cynical about much in government, yes. We were skeptical about many government programs, yes. We thought ourselves the watchdogs of government, yes. We delighted in exposes of bungling and corruption, yes. But enemies of government? No.

In any event I don't recall hearing much in those days about the "adversary relationship" between press and government. Today I hear the phrase everywhere.

It reflects an attitude that shows in many ways. At these new-style press conferences, including those of the President, the questions often seem less designed to elicit information than to entrap. Even the daily press briefings by Jody Powell have become a sort of duel, an encounter that would have astonished Steve Early and the then White House press regulars.

There appears to be a widespread view that here on one side are we, the press, and over there on the other side are government officials, none of whom can be trusted.

I suppose it's a result of Watergate. We blame everything now on Watergate—much as the Chinese do everything on the Gang of Four.

But it is, I must confess to you, an attitude that leaves me uneasy.

Under our Constitution the three official Estates of the realm are the executive, the legislature, and the judiciary. Each has a different role and sometimes they disagree, one with another, about what is proper public policy. But no one supposes that because a President may differ with Congress on a particular matter that they are "enemies" by nature, or that the Supreme Court is an adversary of both.

Unless each gives the others a full measure of respect our society would dissolve into anarchy.

The press is not an institution of government. But it is most definitely an institution of our society, made so by the First Amendment to our Constitution. It is not too much to say, I think, that one intent of the First Amendment was to make the press, collectively, a part of the system of checks and balances that helps preserve a free society.

That is, in Macaulay's felicitous phrase, we in the press constitute a Fourth Estate of the realm. But that very phrase "Fourth Estate" implies that we are part of the self-governing process of our society, not something set apart from it.

As such we are permitted—nay, invited—to inform the people what the other Estates are doing and upon occasion to criticize what they are doing. In that last respect, of course, our right is not different from that of other citizens, all of whom are free to speak their minds. We differ from other citizens only in the fact that watching government perform is our full-time occupation.

But that role, or so it seems to me, is not the same thing as casting ourselves as adversaries, enemies even, of government as government. There's a distinction, and an important one, between differing with *a* President in some editorial or commentary and being an adversary of *the* Presidency.

To think ourselves adversaries of government as government makes me uneasy for several reasons. For one, if the press collectively thinks itself an adversary of government, why would not the government begin to think of itself as adversary to the press?

We have, in fact, already seen some signs of that. Some of us have been spied upon—our mail opened, our telephones tapped—as if we were agents of some hostile power. Some of us have been hauled into court and thrown into jail.

The reminder here is that in polity, as in physics, every

action creates a reaction. We have in turn reacted to this harassment, as well we should. We ought to cry alarm whenever the government, whether the executive or the judiciary, seems bent on intimidating us by harassment. But we ought also, so I think, take care that we in our turn do not over-react.

We should, with all the energy that is in us, defend the rights of all citizens against executive spying. When citizens cannot write to one another freely or speak to one another without fear, then all liberty is endangered.

We should demand for all citizens due process against unwarranted searches and seizures of their private papers. We should hold both the executive and judiciary strictly accountable that the right of the people be secure in their persons, their houses, papers and effects be not violated.

We should insist that no warrants, or subpoenas, be issued against any citizen except upon probable cause, duly supported before the courts and particularly describing why and what is to be seized.

We should be zealous in our protection of all citizens in their right to a public trial by an impartial jury. That means we should take care that nothing we do prejudices the minds of those who will be called to give judgment on a person accused.

That also means, surely, that we should uphold the right of an accused to obtain witnesses in his favor—by compulsory process, if need be, as the Constitution provides.

We should remember that the First Amendment protects the freedom of speech of all citizens, not just our own voices.

That is where we should stand our ground, defending the rights of all.

Beyond that we should be wary.

We should be especially wary of claiming for ourselves alone any exemption for the obligations of all citizens, including the obligation to bear witness in our courts once due process has been observed.

The risk, if we do, is that someday the people may come to think us arrogant. For there is nothing in any part of the Bill of Rights, including the First Amendment, that makes us a privileged class apart.

And it cannot be said too often: Freedom of the press is not some immutable right handed down to Moses on Mt. Sinai. It is a political right granted by the people in a political document, and what the people grant they can, if they ever choose, take away.

But what a precious right that is they have granted us.

So long as the First Amendment stands, the American press, each part choosing what it will, can publish what it will. When we think it necessary to the public weal we can seize upon documents taken from government archives and broadcast them to the world. We can strip privacy from the councils of state and from grand juries. We are free to heap criticism not only upon our elected governors but upon all whom chance has made an object of public attention. We can, if we wish, publish even the lascivious and the sadistic. And we can advance any opinion on any subject.

This is unique among the nations of the world. In what other country is the press so free? Even in that England which is the wellspring of our liberties there remain after 200 years limits upon the freedom of the press.

Only in America are the boundaries of that freedom so broad.

That is why I cherish it and pray the people will never think we abuse it. For there is no liberty that cannot be abused and none that cannot be lost.

Finally, let me say that it has been my good fortune to live in such a country, and for more than forty years to have been a small part of its Fourth Estate.

That is, incidentally, longer than any person now serving in the other Estates of the realm, the Supreme Court, the Congress or those Executive Offices on Pennsylvania Avenue. With a little bit of luck I hope to still be speaking my mind when many of those now serving the other Estates have gone on to other occupations.

So there is no other honor I could receive greater than your expression here this evening that, in the opinion of my peers, I have served well that Fourth Estate.

I am grateful to you for this award. And I thank you for listening.

IN DEFENSE OF PRIVILEGE [1]

DANIEL SCHORR [2]

"It is time to take an open-minded look at this gulf of unease and suspicion that has opened between the people and their press." Daniel Schorr, television personality and reporter, announced his objective in a speech to Press-Bar Awards Luncheon of the State Bar of California, meeting at the India Suite, Stanford Court Hotel in San Francisco, December 14, 1978.

In this speech, Schorr reviews the current attacks on the press, mentioning the Nixon-Agnew hostility toward the news media, his own difficulty arising from leaking a confidential document to the *Village Voice* (that caused his dismissal by CBS), the Farber case in which a reporter went to jail for refusing to divulge his sources, and the Supreme Court decision giving the police the right to search a newspaper office for a reporter's notes.

The method of the Schorr's speech is meant to establish identification or consubstantiality (Kenneth Burke's term) between antagonists: reporters and lawyers. Schorr carefully spells out the basic conflict between the two groups and then points out how on the key issue of privacy their positions are analogous and not in conflict. With this stance established, he suggests that they should stand together against attempts to deny protection to reporters who refuse to reveal their sources. The rhetorical movement is finally brought in phase with the sentence: "Fulfillment of our function, like fulfillment of your function, depends on a fragile thing called privilege. . . . There cannot, ultimately, be any victory for a civil liberty at the expense of another civil liberty."

Technically he pursues an axiological rhetoric by attempting to advance his set of human values above those of his listeners from the legal profession. He places more value on the public's "right to know"—the relentless pursuit of the truth—than on security and obedience.

Schorr is known as a fighter and a gadfly. Throughout his

[1] Delivered at Press-Bar Awards Luncheon of the State Bar of California, San Francisco, California, at 12:30 P.M., December 14, 1978. Quoted by permission.

[2] For biographical note, see Appendix.

journalistic career he has made a business out of subjecting the Establishment, wherever it exists, to intense, harsh, and relentless probing. Never timid, he has refused to bend or to be silenced regardless of pressure from his employers, government sources, lawyers, or even colleagues. As a result, he has earned "an impressive list of scoops" (*Current Biography*, February 1978). With "a voice from a gravel pit," he has provided his television listeners with biting, pungent, and revealing reports mainly on CBS News. Since his dismissal by CBS (February 1976), he has reached the public via the lecture circuit and his columns in the Des Moines (Iowa) *Register*.

My subject today is privilege. It is high time for some frank discussion of privilege between lawyers and journalists. Neither of our professions can adequately fulfill its function without it, and both of us face challenges to cherished immunities.

Most people think of privilege in its first dictionary meaning—something enjoyed by the overly advantaged, like "the privileges of the very rich." Then, there are the immunities of government officials, like the President's "executive privilege" and the congressional privilege against being sued for slander for what is said in Congress. You have to read way down to the fourth and fifth definitions before you arrive at the notion of privilege as an immunity available to the unelected to serve our common liberties.

The press claims privilege under the First Amendment, in the interest of an informed public, and that privilege is today under massive attack. The bar, which is playing a role in that attack, enjoys privilege, in the interest of public justice. And the lawyer's privilege (which I know you call the client's privilege) is starting to come under attack, in the press, among other places.

People question a privilege that means that Mark Lane could stay mum about what his clients were brewing in Jonestown, just as people question a privilege that means that Myron Farber could stay mum about aspects of his investigation of mysterious deaths in a hospital in New Jersey.

Neither privilege will survive if it is not defended against waves of emotion and unreason. So, it is time that lawyers and journalists talk to each other.

So far you have been in better shape than we because the rules that protect lawyers are written by lawyers for lawyers and sanctified by other lawyers in judicial robes. When an attorney learned from a client where bodies in unsolved murders lay buried, the bar upheld his right not to communicate this information to the parents of a missing child, and the New York courts upheld the bar.

I must admit to having experienced a severe case of privilege envy when I sat in, last summer, on a meeting of the American Bar Association's commission rewriting the Code of Professional Responsibility. In this meeting (and, exercising the ill-protected journalist's privilege, I shall keep a promise to name no names) commission members admitted that, safe behind the shield of confidentiality, lawyers sometimes counseled their clients on evasion and even violation of the law: A lawyer advised a client to risk proceeding with a building project without waiting for a permit. A lawyer condoned bribes to foreign bureaucrats to expedite a corporate executive's relocation. A lawyer proclaimed, as an act of conscience, having advised a teenager, in violation of the law of that state, to get an abortion without seeking parental consent.

The sacred lawyer-client relationship cloaks all this—in the client's interest, it is said. Yet, sealed lips can part when it suits a lawyer's purpose. Under the lawyer's code, one may reveal a client's secrets when necessary to collect a fee or to defend oneself against a client's accusations. You will recall that F. Lee Bailey invoked that right to counter Patricia Hearst's charge of "incompetent" defense. If correctly quoted, Bailey threatened to reveal actions by Miss Hearst "far more serious than those she has been tried for." That was a little much for the bar commission, which is now planning to amend the code to stipulate that a lawyer "ratting" on a client should not disclose "more than reasonably necessary to the issue."

It is amazing that the lawyer who can spill a client's secrets when his fee is threatened can stay silent when somebody else's life is threatened. Under the code, a lawyer "may" (but does not have to) tell the court of a crime about to be committed. The bar commission was concluding— even before Jonestown—that the time may have come to change that "may" to "must." The bar is beginning to feel a chill breeze of public disapproval of the price of privilege.

But nothing—not yet anyway—like the Arctic storms that rage around the press. The courts today are on what can only be described as a rampage against the news media. They have given their blessing to police searches of newsrooms, to restriction of coverage of courtroom proceedings, and to enforcement by contempt orders of demands for confidential notes and sources. Going after reporters is becoming a national legal sport, almost a routine like a motion to dismiss. The Reporters' Committee for Freedom of the Press says that subpoenas on reporters, a rarity before 1968, jumped to about 150 in the two years starting in 1968, and to about 500 in the six years after 1970. Then, the committee stopped counting. It can't keep track any more.

All in the name of justice. But there seems to be a special zest in the judicial jabbing at the press. In New Jersey, District Court Judge Frederick Lacey gratuitously described Myron Farber as "standing on an altar of greed" in resisting demands for his notes and sources. The chief justice, Warren Burger, reportedly expressed his glee that Farber had gone to jail. In upholding the First Amendment right of a Boston bank to engage in corporate spending on an issue on the election ballot, Burger seized the opportunity to inveigh against "the modern media empires" exercising an "unfair advantage" in terms of "corporate domination of the political process."

Clearly Justice Burger is not alone in his hostility to the news media. Indeed, he seems to be riding some popular wave of resentment. The courts follow not just the election returns. They move, in a general way, with the

mood of the times, and that mood is increasingly anti-press.
It has taken me a long time, perhaps because of a journalist's thick skin, but it is finally getting home to me
that Americans don't love the press. They may like some
of us personally, and they may be fascinated by those they
see on television, but they are not enamored of us as an
institution.

It seemed only an aberration of Nixon times when Vice
President Agnew, in 1969, attacked a "tiny and closed fra-
ternity of privileged men" and produced more than a
hundred-thousand supportive letters and telegrams to the
networks. When I found myself, in 1976, more reviled than
praised for assisting the public to get a suppressed congressional report, I thought that might be an exceptional
circumstance having to do with my "abrasive personality."
Since then, however, the signs of anti-press sentiment have
become more general and more alarming.

No mass picket lines of outraged citizens formed outside
the Hackensack courthouse when Myron Farber went to
jail. And many Americans seem ready to believe—so soon
after Watergate!—that reporters endanger national security
by finding out about things the government calls secret.
This despite the fact that the most outrageous security
violations have nothing to do with the press. Like Ambassador Graham Martin, bitter about Viet Nam, roaming
around North Carolina with a trunkful of secret documents
that got lost with his stolen car. Like the CIA letting a
dozen copies of its hottest spy satellite manual wander
away, one to be sold to the Russians, unmissed for months
until the CIA heard from the FBI. Like a CIA analyst
passing top-secret documents to Senator Henry Jackson's
staff to help fight an arms-control treaty. Traveling around
the country, I am rarely asked about these things, but I am
frequently asked whether the press doesn't spill too many
secrets and whether it hasn't become too powerful altogether for the general good.

It's an interesting development, if you're interested in

semantics, that "Power of the press" used to be a white-hat phrase, but the more recent "Power of the news media" emerges with a black-hat connotation. "The Bad News Media" is a game that any number in any position can play. It makes soulmates of a Carter and a Nixon. Nixon's former speech-writer, Ray Price, talks of the "sustaining venom of the media," and Jody Powell, Jimmy Carter's press secretary, sneers at "the imperial press." In his recent interview with Bill Moyers on public television, President Carter talked about "the irresponsibility of the press." Bert Lance, now under grand jury investigation, says he has been the victim of "careless, erroneous or biased reporting" of a kind that could lead to censorship in this country, and he finds himself strumming a chord of popular sentiment. We are getting to the point where a politician will be able to run against the news media as he used to run against communism, crime or corruption—issues no longer available to some of them.

The press may be a fair target, but it is being hit with the wrong ammunition. There are dangers in a situation where the press, instead of being criticized, is turned into the enemy. If the press becomes totally discredited, its ability to fulfill its function of watchdog for the public will be destroyed. Nixon, as Bill Safire has candidly written about his former boss, considered the press his enemy and mounted a conspiracy against it. To discredit the press was a necessary part of maintaining a coverup.

Let me say that I can understand, from personal experience, that one can get mad at the press sometimes. One need only to be on the other side of the fence, to be involved in a public controversy or to be interviewed for *Sixty Minutes,* and one is in danger of being converted from an advocate of Freedom *of* the Press to a crusader for Freedom *from* the Press. Two weeks ago I found myself in trouble with a lot of people whose respect I value because the Associated Press misquoted me as saying that the late Representative Leo Ryan was my source in uncovering the

CIA operation in Angola. I had said, in extemporaneous remarks at the Naval War College, that Ryan thought Angola was a terrible idea and was determined that it should be exposed. But since I had nothing to do with uncovering Angola, Ryan could not have been my source. It turned out the AP had gotten its story from a young reporter for the Providence *Journal,* who misunderstood me. In fact, she had come up after my speech to ask whether she had it straight that Ryan had given me the report of the Pike committee. She ended up still not getting it straight, and I ended up with a lot of angry and puzzled people around the country who had remembered me as devoted to the protection of my sources. Which I still am.

I am also still a reporter, in love with my profession. But I think that it is time to take an open-minded look at this gulf of unease and suspicion that has opened between the people and their press. I have no final answers, but I have some tentative thoughts, and they have to do with the evolution of the press, both in terms of economic concentration of newspapers and the development of a television industry that subordinates the reporter to a large entertainment enterprise, an enterprise that is widely perceived as exploiting violence, sex, and audience susceptibilities for bigger ratings and greater profits.

To defend the First Amendment today, one must defend not only the brave reporter uncovering wrongdoing, but *Hustler* magazine uncovering . . . well, you name it. It was a First Amendment victory when a federal judge in Miami dismissed a $25-million suit by a teenager convicted of murder who said he had learned it from television, but it didn't help our case with the public that the judge said violence is "one of the disadvantages the First Amendment requires that we live with." This kind of case seems far removed from the original role of the reporter, whose image is also changing.

Once, a reporter was perceived as a relentless and usually impecunious pursuer of the truth. Today, the reporter is, often as not, perceived as the well-heeled and arrogant offspring of a giant amusement industry. The journalist appears on the tube as lost in the wasteland blur among the prime-time programmers, the docu-drama titillators, the happy-news chucklers and the Saturday morning sugar-plugging hucksters. It seems a long way from John Peter Zenger of colonial times, or even from Hildy Johnson of "The Front Page."

The press, once typically anti-establishment, is perceived now as itself a huge establishment. The picture of a great faceless corporation, manipulating tastes, brainwashing audiences, making and breaking public figures is hard to reconcile with a band of gallant gadflies, exposing the corrupt and powerful, goading the pompous, and deserving of special legal privilege so that they can wage our war for truth.

"The press," wrote Justice Douglas, "has a preferred position in our constitutional scheme, not to enable it to make money, not to set newsmen apart as a favored class, but to bring fulfillment to the public's right to know."

If we could somehow convince the public that it is their right to know that is primarily involved in what we do, I think we would have better luck defending our privilege. But it is getting harder and harder to do.

That being so, you lawyers have us at a disadvantage. There has always been tension between the two great principles of free press and fair trial, requiring sensitive balancing, but, under present conditions, the balance is getting tipped toward an extreme anti-press position. The message of the Supreme Court's *Branzburg-Caldwell* decision, that invasion of the province of the free press is something to be done reluctantly and rarely when there is no other way, is being lost. An angrier and less sensitive judge acted summarily against Farber and the New York *Times* without even bothering to ascertain whether Farber's notes had any relevance to the defense.

It may give judges, prosecutors, and defense lawyers

some satisfaction to see unyielding reporters go to jail. And, if reporters go on trying to do their job, there will be many of them in jail. Journalism may become, for some, a form of civil disobedience. But I urge you to consider the nature of the Pyrrhic victory that you will win if you press your current advantage too far. It is your press, too, and it stood you in good stead when the Nixon coverup had justice paralyzed.

It is only six years since Watergate, and I wonder what the situation would be today if a vast coverup conspiracy were in progress. With confidential sources in danger, would there be a Deep Throat to blow the whistle? With reporters facing some future jail term for contempt, would there be a reporter to write the story? With the possibility of newsroom searches and ruinous fines for contempt, could you count on every paper, magazine, and broadcaster to put out the story?

I urge you to consider the larger consequences of drying up confidential sources and giving reporters their come-uppance, making it easier for those in authority to manage the news. Our news media can be arrogant, affluent, sex-prone, violence-prone, and sometimes downright smug. But it is the only press we have, and at crucial times has helped to save our free institutions.

Fulfillment of our function, like fulfillment of your function, depends on a fragile thing called privilege. Ours today is more fragile than yours, but yours is also being questioned. Privilege ultimately rests on society's recognition of its value. We live in times of passion when many values are being challenged. If the Free Press is eroded in the name of Justice, then Justice will surely be eroded next. There cannot, ultimately, be any victory for a civil liberty at the expense of another civil liberty.

APPENDIX

BIOGRAPHICAL NOTES

BEGIN, MENACHEM (1913–   ). Born, Brest-Litovsk, Poland (now Soviet Union) ; J. M., University of Warsaw, 1935; head of Betar Zionist Youth Movement in Poland, 1939; arrested and held in concentration camp in Siberia, 1940–41; settled in Palestine, 1942; leader of underground Irgun Zvai Leumi, 1943–48; founder (now chairman), Herut (Freedom) Movement in Israel, 1948–   ; member of Knesset (parliament), 1948–   ; minister without portfolio, 1967–70; prime minister, 1977–   ; awarded Nobel Peace Prize with Sadat, 1978; author: *Ha-Mered* (1950), *Be-Leilot* (1953), the *Revolt* (1964), *The White Nights* (1957) (See also *Current Biography: October* 1977.)

BELL, GRIFFIN B. (1918–   ). Born, Americus, Georgia; student, Georgia Southwest College; LL.B., cum laude, Mercer University, 1948, LL.D, 1967; admitted to Georgia bar, 1947; practiced law in Savannah and Rome, Georgia, 1947–53; King and Spalding, Atlanta, 1953–61; 1976; US judge, Fifth Circuit Court, 1961–76; US Attorney General, 1977–   ; major, US Army, 1941–46; order of Coif (See also *Current Biography: June* 1977.)

BOWEN, WILLIAM G. (1933–   ). Born, Cincinnati, Ohio; B.A., Denison University, 1955; Ph.D., Princeton University, 1958; assistant professor of economics, Princeton University, 1958–61; associate professor, 1961–65; professor, 1965–   ; director of graduate studies, Woodrow Wilson School of Public and International Affairs, Princeton, 1964–66; provost, 1967–72; president, 1972–   ; Ford Foundation Faculty Research Fellowship, 1966–67; board of directors of American Council on Education, (chairman, 1968), and the Association of American Universities, trustee, Alfred P. Sloan Foundation, director of NCR Corp., 1975–   ; author: *The Wage-Price Issue; A Theoretical Analysis* (1960), *Wage Behavior in the Post-war Period: An Empirical Analysis* (1960), *Economic Aspects of Education* (1964), *The Federal Government and Princeton University* (1962), *Labor and the National Economy* (1964), *The Economics of Labor Force Participation* (with T. A. Finegan) (1969), and *Performing Arts: The Economic Dilemma* (with W. J. Baumol) (1966), *Economic Pressures on Major University* (1969) ; member, Phi Beta Kappa, Sigma Chi, American Academy of Arts and Sciences and the American Economic Association.

BROWN, JERRY (Edmund G. Brown Jr.) (1938–   ). Born, San Francisco, California; B.A., University of California at Berkeley, 1961; J.D., Yale University, 1964; admitted to California bar, 1965; research attorney, California Supreme Court, 1964–65; member of law firm of Tuttle & Taylor, Los Angeles, 1966–69; secretary of state, 1971–75; governor of California, 1975–   (See also *Current Biography: April* 1975.)

BRZEZINSKI, ZBIGNIEW (1928–   ). Born, Warsaw, Poland; B.A., McGill University, 1949, M.A., 1950; Ph.D., Harvard University, 1953; honorary degrees, Alliance College, 1966; College of the Holy Cross, 1971; came to US in 1953; naturalized 1958; instructor, Russian Research Center, Harvard University, 1953–56; assistant professor, 1956–60; associate professor, Columbia University, 1960–62; professor, 1962–77; member of faculty Russian Institute, 1960–77; director, Trilateral Commission, 1973–76; assistant to President Carter for National Security Affairs, 1977–   ; Guggenheim Fellowship, 1960; Ford Foundation Grant, 1970; Fellow, American Academy of Arts and Sciences; author, *Political Controls in the Soviet Army* (1954), *The Permanent Purge-Politics in Soviet Totalitarianism* (1956), *The Soviet Bloc: Unity and Conflict* (1960); *Ideology and Power in Soviet Politics* (1962); *Alternative to Partition* (1965); *Between Two Ages* (1970); *The Fragile Blossom* (1971); numerous articles on comparative government and international affairs (See also *Current Biography: April* 1970.)

BURGER, WARREN E (ARL) (1907–   ). Born, St. Paul, Minnesota; student, University of Minnesota, 1925–27; LL.B., magna cum laude, St. Paul College of Law (now William Mitchell College of Law); Doctor of Laws, 1931; honorary degrees, LL.D., William Mitchell College of Law, 1966, and New York Law School, 1976; admitted to Minnesota bar, 1931; faculty, William Mitchell College of Law, 1931–53; partner, Faricy, Burger, Moore & Costello (and predecessor firms), 1935–53; assistant attorney general in charge of Civil Division, US Department of Justice, 1953–56; judge of US Court of Appeals, District of Columbia, 1956–69; Chief Justice of the United States, 1969–   ; lecturer, American and European law schools; faculty, Appellate Judges Seminar, New York University Law School, 1958–   ; member and legal adviser to US delegation to International Labor Organization, Geneva, 1954; contributor to law journals and other publications. (See also *Current Biography: November 1969.*)

BUSH, GEORGE HERBERT WALKER (1924–   ). Born, Milton, Massachusetts; B.A., Yale University, 1948; honorary degrees,

Adelphi University, Austin College, Northern Michigan University, Franklin Pierce College, Allegheny College; Zapata Petroleum Corporation, 1953–66; US House of Representatives, 1967–1971; ambassador to United Nations, 1971–72; Chairman, Republican National Committee, 1973–74; chief US Liaison Office, Peking, People's Republic of China, 1974–75; director, Central Intelligence Agency, 1976–77; US Naval Reserve, World War II (See also *Current Biography: January* 1972.)

CARTER, JIMMY (James Earl Carter Jr.) (1924–   ). Born, Plains, Georgia; student, Georgia Southwestern University, 1941–42; Georgia Institute of Technology, 1942–43; B.S., US Naval Academy, 1946; postgraduate instruction, nuclear physics, Union College, 1952; US Navy, 1947–53, advancing through grades to lieutenant commander; resigned 1953; farmer, warehouseman, 1953–77; served two terms in Georgia senate (Democrat), 1962–66 (voted most effective member); governor, 1971–74; chairman, Democratic National Campaign Committee, 1974; elected President, 1976; inaugurated, January 20, 1977; past president, Georgia Planning Association; first chairman, West Central Georgia Planning and Development Commission; former chairman, Sumter County Board of Education; district governor, Lions International; state chairman, March of Dimes; author, *Why Not the Best*, 1975. (See also *Current Biography: November 1977*.)

CHURCH, FRANK (1924–   ). Born, Boise, Idaho; on debating team, Boise high school; B.A., Stanford University, 1947; LL.B., 1950; admitted to Idaho bar, 1950; practiced law in Boise, 1950–56; Idaho chairman, Crusade for Freedom, 1954, 1955; keynote speaker, state Democratic convention, 1952; member, US Senate (Democrat, Idaho), 1957–   ; member, Senate Committee on Foreign Relations; Senate Committee on Interior and Insular Affairs; Senate Special Committee on Aging; chairman, Senate Select Committee on Intelligence; keynote speaker, Democratic National Convention, 1960; US Army, World War II; elected one of Ten Outstanding Young Men of 1957, US Junior Chamber of Commerce; recipient, American Legion Oratorical Contest Award, 1941 ("The American Way of Life"); Joffre Debate Medal, Stanford University, 1947; member, Phi Beta Kappa. (See also *Current Biography: March 1978*.)

DUBOS, RENÉ J. (1901–   ). Born, Saint-Brice-sous-Forêt, France; student, College Chaptal, Paris, 1915–19; Institut National Agronomique, Paris, 1919–21; served in French army, 1921–22; assistant, editorial staff, International Institute of Agriculture, Rome, 1922–24; came to United States, 1924; naturalized, 1938; research assistant, soil microbiology, New Jersey Experimental

Station, Rutgers University, 1924–27; Ph.D., Rutgers University, 1927; fellow, Rockefeller Institute of Medical Research, 1927–28; assistant, 1928–30; associate, 1930–38; associate member, 1938–41; member, 1941–42, 1944–56; George Fabyan Professor of Comparative Pathology and Professor of Tropical Medicine, Harvard Medical School, 1942–44; member and professor, Rockefeller University for Medical Research, 1957–71; recipient of twenty-six honorary degrees and numerous awards; author, *The Bacterial Cell*, 1945; *Man Adapting*, 1965; *So Human an Animal* (Pulitzer Prize) , 1968; *A God Within*, 1972; and other works. (See also *Current Biography: January 1973*.)

FRANKLIN, BARBARA HACKMAN (1940–   ) . Born, Lancaster, Pennsylvania; B.S., Pennsylvania State University, 1962; M.B.A., Harvard Business School, 1964; honorary degree, D.Sc., Bryant College, 1973; Singer Co., 1964–68; Vice President, First National City Bank, New York, 1969–71; Assistant to US President, 1971–73; Commissioner Consumer Product Safety Commission, 1973–   .

GRIFFIN, ROBERT P. (1923–   ) . Born, Traverse City, Michigan. A.B., B.S., Central Michigan University, 1947, LL.D., 1963; J.D., University of Michigan, 1950; honorary degrees from eleven institutions; admitted to Michigan bar, 1950; practiced law, Traverse City, 1950–56; member, US House of Representatives, 1957–65 (Republican, Michigan) ; member US Senate, 1966–78; US Army.

HANLEY, JOHN W. (1922–   ) . Born, Parkersburg, West Virginia; B.S., Pennsylvania State University, 1942; M.B.A., Harvard University, 1947; Honoris Causa, University of Missouri-Rolla, 1974; Allegheny Ludlum Steel Corp., 1942–43; Procter & Gamble, 1947–69; Monsanto Company, 1969; president, 1972–   ; director of several corporations and institutions.

McGILL, WILLIAM JAMES (1922–   ) . Born, New York City; A.B., Fordham College, 1943; M.A., 1947; Ph.D., Harvard University, 1953; instructor, Fordham University, 1947–48; teaching fellow, Harvard University, 1949–50; instructor, Boston College, 1950–51; staff member, Lincoln Laboratory (MIT) , 1951–54; assistant professor, Massachusetts Institute of Technology, 1954–56; assistant professor, Columbia University, 1956–58; associate professor, 1958–60; professor, 1960–65; professor, University of California, San Diego, 1965–68; chancellor, 1968–70; president, Columbia University, 1970–   ; fellow, American Association for the Advancement of Science, 1963; American Psychological Association, 1967; board of trustees, Psychometric Society, 1967–   ;

associate editor, *Journal of Mathematical Psychology,* 1964– ,
Perception and Psychophysics, 1966–70; consulting editor, *Psychological Bulletin,* 1966–70; *Psychometrika,* 1965–70; published
over 35 studies and reviews; member, Phi Beta Kappa, Sigma Xi;
Achievement Award of Fordham University, 1968. (See also *Current Biography: June 1971.*)

MATHIAS, CHARLES McCURDY, JR. (1922–). Born, Frederick, Maryland; US Navy, 1942–46; B.A., Haverford College,
1944; LL.B., University of Maryland, 1949; partner, Mathias,
Mathias & Michel, Frederick, 1949–53; assistant attorney general
of Maryland, 1953–54; city attorney, Frederick, 1954–59; member,
House of Delegates, Maryland, 1958; partner, Niles, Barton,
Markell and Gans, Baltimore, 1960– ; member, US House of
Representatives (Republican, Maryland), 1961–67; US Senate,
1968– . (See also *Current Biography: December 1972.*)

MUSKIE, EDMUND SIXTUS (1914–). Born, Rumford, Maine;
A.B., Bates College, 1936; LL.B., Cornell University, 1939; honorary degrees, Colby College, Bates College, Bowdoin College,
Suffolk University, University of Maine, Portland University;
admitted to Massachusetts bar, 1939; admitted to Maine bar,
1940; practiced law, Waterville, Maine, 1940, 1945–55; governor
of Maine, 1955–59; US Senate, 1959– ; Democratic candidate
for Vice President, US, 1968; US Naval Reserve, 1942–45; author:
Journeys (1972); member, Phi Beta Kappa (See also *Current
Biography, December* 1968.)

ROYSTER, VERMONT CONNECTICUT (1914–). Born, Raleigh,
North Carolina; A.B., University of North Carolina, 1935; LL.D.,
1959; honorary degrees, Temple University, Elon College, Colby
College; New York City News Bureau, 1936; *Wall Street Journal,*
1936– ; editor, 1958–71; contributing columnist, 1971– ;
William Rand Kenan professor of Journalism and Public Affairs,
University of North Carolina, Chapel Hill, 1971– ; commentator public affairs CBS radio and TV, 1972–77; numerous journalism awards including Pulitzer prize for editorial writing, 1953;
author: (with others) *Main Street and Beyond* (1959), *Journey
Through the Soviet Union* (1962), *A Pride of Prejudices* (1967);
US Naval Reserve, 1940–45; member, Phi Beta Kappa.

SADAT, ANWAR EL- (1918–). Born, Talah, province of
Monufiya, Egypt; Abbassia Military Academy, 1936–38 (graduated); imprisoned for nationalist activities, 1942–49; editor, *Al
Gomhuriya,* 1955–56; minister of State of Egypt, 1954–56; vicechairman, National Assembly 1957–60; chairman, 1960–68; gen-

eral secretary, Egyptian National Union, 1957–61, chairman, Afro-Asian Solidarity Conference, 1958; speaker, United Arab Republic Assembly 1961–69; presidential council 1962–64; vice-president of Egypt, 1964–67; 1969–70; interim president, 1970; president of council, Federation of Arab Republics 1970–   ; awarded Nobel Peace Prize with Begin, 1978; author, *Revolt on Nile* (1957), *In Search of Identity* (1978), (See also *Current Biography: March* 1971).

SCHORR, DANIEL LOUIS (1916–   ). Born, New York City; B.S.S., College of the City of New York, 1939; editor, Jewish Telegraphic Agency, 1939–41; news editor, ANETA (Netherlands) News Agency, N.Y., 1941–48; free lance correspondent, N.Y. *Times, Christian Science Monitor, London Daily Mail,* 1948–53; CBS News, 1953–1976; Regents professor, U. of California, 1977; author: *Don't Get Sick in America* (1971), *Clearing the Air* (1977); recipient of many awards including the Emmy for coverage of Watergate scandal, 1972, 1973, 1974; US Army, 1943–45 (See also *Current Biography, February* 1978.)

STEVENSON, ADLAI EWING III (1930–   ). Born Chicago, Illinois; A.B., Harvard University, 1957; LL.B., 1957; admitted to Illinois bar, 1957; with Mayer, Friedlich, Spiess, Tierney, Brown and Platt, Chicago, 1958–67; Illinois House of Representatives, 1965–67; state treasurer, 1967–70; US Senate, 1970–   ; US Marine Corps Reserve, 1952–54 (See also *Current Biography: April* 1974.)

CUMULATIVE AUTHOR INDEX

1970-1971—1978-1979

A cumulative author index to the volumes of REPRESENTATIVE AMERICAN SPEECHES for the years 1937-1938 through 1959-1960 appears in the 1959-1960 volume and for the years 1960-1961 through 1969-1970 in the 1969-1970 volume.